THE GOLDEN ALBATROSS

ALBATROSS

HOW TO DETERMINE IF YOUR PENSION IS *WORTH IT*

GRUMPUS MAXIMUS

With Foreword by Doug Nordman
Author of *The Military Guide*

ISBN: 978-0-9600589-8-3 (Paperback) 978-0-9600589-9-0 (Hardcover)

Library of Congress Number: 2020933809

The views presented in this book are those of the author and do not necessarily represent the views of DoD or its components.

All content reflects our opinion at a given time and can change as time progress. All information should be taken as an opinion and should not be misconstrued for professional or legal advice. The contents of this book are informational in nature and are not legal or tax advice, and the authors and publishers are not engaged in the provision of legal, tax, or any other advice.

Cover and Book Design by Giada Mannino
Illustrations by Nikolett Mérész

Printed by Choose FI Media, Inc. in the United States of America.

First printing edition 2020.

Choose FI Media, Inc.
P.O. Box 3982
Glen Allen, VA 23058

www.choosefi.com
grumpusmaximus.com

Dedication

For Mrs. Grumpus and the two Grumpus Minimi (min-EE-my).
Without them I'd be twice as sane, but my life would be four
times as boring.

Thanks

Most books aren't written by just one person. There's usually a team behind the author. This book is no exception. I'd like to thank Chris Pascale for his numerous edits and guidance. Not only did he edit and format early versions of my book, but he let me learn from his mistakes as an author. If you're interested in a warrior poet's take on many of the military, mental health, and financial themes I address in this book, you should check out his book *War Poems: A Marine's Tour 2003-2008*.

I'd also like to thank Doug Nordman for his encouragement. He never doubted I would write this book. I'd also like to thank him for his publishing, editing, and general guidance. Doug is the original military-focused Financial Independence (FI) blogger and author. The rest of us, me included, are just following in his footsteps. If you're in the military and interested in achieving FI, his blog, The Military Guide, is a must-read.

My father also deserves a big "Thank You." He's like Jack the Ripper with a red pen and spent many days editing earlier versions of this book. His grasp of the minute and mundane rules of the English language made this book presentable enough to convince my eventual publisher to take it seriously. That's definitely worth a case of good beer the next time I see him.

Speaking of my publisher, I'd like to thank MK Williams for all the time she spent taking my initial submission and turning it into something that's publisher worthy. Other than name dropping Doug Nordman in my initial email to her, she didn't know me from Adam. That said, she took this project seriously from the moment my first email hit her inbox and never let up. Although she's fond of pointing out that I approached her with an almost complete book, the version you're reading today is head and shoulders better than where we started. That is a direct result of her guidance, encouragement, optimism, and drive. If you're sitting on a manuscript, or even just a book idea, and you don't know what to do, contact her. She's earned the Grumpus Maximus official seal of approval.

Conversely, a small "thank you" to my parents' neighbor. Several years ago, while I was on leave, I told you I might like to write for a living. You responded with an extremely skeptical, "So, you think you can write?" Your skepticism coupled with my need to prove you wrong motivated me during many a late-night writing session to see this project through to the end.

Finally, I need to thank my friend that I reference in Chapter 1. Without her encouragement to start my blog, this book would have never materialized. It's important to have a friend who will call B.S. and who isn't afraid to disagree with your point of view—especially when writing a book. Her strength and tenacity in the face of some of life's most serious challenges continues to amaze and buoy me whenever I'm down.

Contents

Foreword ii

Preface iv

How to Use This Book viii

Introduction xii

PART 1

1 What is a Golden Albatross? 1

2 Worth vs. Worth It 9

3 Why Would One Stay? 19

4 Gutting It Out 29

5 The Opposite of Gutting It Out 41

6 Mental Health, Sad Work, and Stuff 53

PART 2

7 Is Your Pension Safe? 69

8 What's Your Pension Worth? 81

9 How to Determine Your Pension's Total Dollar Value (TDV) 102

10 How to Use This New-Found Knowledge 126

11 How to Value Pension Subsidized Healthcare 135

PART 3

12 The Grumpmatic and Mathemagical Comparison Methods 147

13 A Golden Albatross Decision Aid 161

14 Putting It All Together, The Golden Albatross Financial Philosophy 167

Foreword

I've known Grumpus Maximus for several years, and I tremendously enjoy his pension analysis. In the early 1990s I encountered the same career issue: was it worth sticking around to vest in the pension, or was there a better way? Back then (at the dawn of the Web) I had poor access to information and data. I was overworked and exhausted by chronic fatigue. I could have networked to find the people with the knowledge I sought, but I never thought to ask my co-workers where to learn more.

I didn't make the time (or even find the mental bandwidth) to analyze the problem. Instead, overwhelmed by my self-imposed ignorance and fear, I defaulted to the "safe choice": to gut it out for the pension. I spent eight more years living with a miserable work/life balance for what seemed to be the best option.

Nearly a decade later, my spouse confronted the same issue in her career. This time we were able to find more information and talk with the right people. She made the decision to leave her career, go part-time, and find a better path to a pension at an older age. The week she left her full-time job, our quality of life skyrocketed. She knew she made the right choice.

In 2002 I vested in my pension and retired. After a few months (when

I caught up on sleep and my head cleared) I checked my math. We had not only reached financial independence, but we had way overshot the mark. We had more money than we needed.

Today I'd trade a million dollars of my net worth to go back in time and make a different decision. That's why I advise people to stay in their careers as long as they're feeling challenged and fulfilled. You might not be tap-dancing to work every day like Warren Buffett, but you should be feeling generally satisfied and even happy. When the fun stops, then it's time for a career decision which might cost your pension: what's it worth, and is it worth the sacrifice?

Grumpus has the tools to help you find your answer, but you have to make the time (and find the mental bandwidth) to use them now. If the crisis ever comes, you'll be glad that you already analyzed your options. After you finish this book, I highly recommend the links to Grumpus's community. You can use his social network to research your answers, and you'll get great advice from people who have already been through your situation. Before you gut it out, know what your pension is worth— and whether it's *worth it*.

– Doug Nordman

Preface

The *Golden Albatross* has landed in book format! Welcome to my book, I am the author Grumpus Maximus—father, husband, blogger, hobby horticulturalist, and retired service member.

Thanks for reading this far, and before you leave, let me tell you why I wrote this book. I wrote this book to help people in pensionable career fields decide if staying for the pension (i.e. gutting it out) is *worth it*. Thus, I primarily wrote this book with future pensioners in mind. However, as I've discovered through feedback from my blog, large compensation as an enticement to stay towards the end of an employee's career isn't limited to pensionable career fields. In either case, staying to earn that pension (or that major monetary compensation) may not be in the employee's best interest.

Why? My personal experience and the research connected to my blogging lead me to believe that many future pensioners currently work in career fields that demand more of them than *normal* careers. In the public sector, these workers include teachers, firefighters, police, city workers, and military members. In the private sector, these are unionized physical jobs like plumbers, electricians, or auto workers. At some point prior to earning the pension, these careers may demand too much of an individual.

Illustration: Grumpus Maximus and the Albatross

On the other hand, the financial stability the pension offers makes walking away, before earning that pension, difficult. Left unresolved, the tension between these two opposing forces can lead to serious problems in a person's life. It did in mine.

Unbeknownst to most of my colleagues and peers, in the spring of 2016 (at 17 years of military service) I suffered a mental breakdown[1] and was diagnosed with mixed depressive-anxiety disorder. Both my depression and anxiety were linked to Post-Traumatic Stress (PTS) caused by several events from earlier in my career. A number of my PTS symptoms centered on how I felt about my profession. By that point, I no longer enjoyed the military. Somewhere between 2012 and 2016 it stopped being my calling in life and turned into...just a job—albeit an extremely demanding one. As a result, when I broke down in 2016, I wanted to resign my commission.

However, if you know anything about U.S. military pensions for personnel who joined in the late 1990s as I did, it's an all-or-nothing Defined Benefit Pension (DBP) bestowed at no less than 20 years of service. I had worked too hard and sacrificed too much to walk away from what could be millions of dollars' worth of retirement pay and medical benefits. Thus, I felt like I was trapped until my 20 years were up.

I've appropriated a term from the Internet and redefined it to describe this inflection point. I call it the *Golden Albatross*. That term represents both the blessing and the curse that is a DBP, which I will explain in detail throughout this book.

Golden Albatross inflection points differ from person-to-person depending on the circumstances. To be honest, I handled mine extremely poorly. There are much better ways to navigate such a meaningful moment than trying to ignore it until you mentally breakdown. In fact, as a result of my blogging and my breakdown, I've developed some distinct methods to help people handle it. It's nothing fancy—mostly common sense and a little bit of math.

Whereas many bloggers write about all the awesome things they got right, and how anyone can achieve the same results if they only pay $39.99 for an all-access pass, I tend to write about what I got wrong both mentally and fiscally during my pensionable career. Think of it as me telling you what to avoid, as opposed to what you should do. More importantly, I give that information away for free.

Why a book, then? Well, since starting the blog, numerous readers have stated they wished my blog content was available in book format. I can identify with the sentiment. I learn best by reading books myself. Therefore, this book represents my first attempt to curate some of the thematic content from my blog in an easily digestible and useable format.

I chose to start with the inflection point of the *Golden Albatross* because from that decision all other content on my blog flows. If a person can't make it past the decision to stay or leave a pensionable career, then it makes no sense to create Financial Independence (FI) plans using a pension as its foundation—which makes up the other part of my blog.

Now, if you're a person who has already decided to stay in a pensionable career, don't worry, there's still content in this book worth reviewing. Furthermore, future books will concentrate on how to use a pension to achieve FI based on the foundations I cover in this book. As a result, I believe this book holds value for anyone in a pensionable career. I hope you feel the same as you read it.

---

[1] I realize that the term "mental breakdown" is loaded with stigma, and has neither a clinical nor a commonly agreed definition. It can (and does) mean anything to anyone. However, I'm not here to fix that problem. All I can say is that I am not ashamed that I had a breakdown, and it's something I talk about openly and freely in my work and home life—specifically because I want to help end that stigma. As a result, it's a term I use comfortably throughout this book, even if it's not clinically correct. If nothing else, consider my use of the term as a talking point with friends, families, co-workers, and medical professionals concerning the psychological hazards connected to many pensionable jobs.

How to Use This Book

In an ideal world, a person would use this book to prepare well in advance of their *Golden Albatross* moment. If that's you, congratulations! You stand to get the most out of this. Read it cover to cover, highlight it, and tab it out. Return to it often because I believe it will serve you well.

However, life isn't usually that simple. Most people don't possess the foresight to prepare for an inflection point like the *Golden Albatross*. I know I didn't. When it happened, I was stuck trying to figure things out on my own. It's probably safe to say that a lot of people have found themselves in a similar situation. Fortunately, this book can be used if you're at that point too. In the military, we'd call it an Emergency Action Plan (EAP). I'm not sure what you'd call it in the civilian world— an outline or road map?

Whether you're reading this book early or late in your career, you'll notice it comes replete with visual aids, math formulas, and stories to help a person figure out two distinct things:

1. What their pension is worth.

2. Whether or not staying for the pension is *worth it*.

Together they make up what I call the *worth vs. worth it* equation.

Illustration: Is your pension worth it?

It's important to note that this is a two-sided equation. One side is subjective. It centers around questions like "What do you value most in this world?" or "What do you value more, x or y?" For instance, do you value time spent with your kids as they grow up more than the promise of financial stability later in life? Alternatively, how important is your physical and/or mental health to you later in life?

There is no *correct* answer to a question like that. Everyone will answer differently based on their set of beliefs and values. However, no matter the answer, a person needs a way to identify, and hopefully quantify, those answers in relation to the mathematical value of the future pension. The first part of this book provides you some techniques to do just that.

The other side of the equation is the mathematical calculation of your pension's monetary value in the future. Even if you're not great at math, it's easy enough to figure out, and a rather straightforward process. There's no voodoo involved, but depending on your pension it might require some educated guesswork. The second part of this book will walk you through that process.

The third part of the book ties the above two sections together with practical examples and visual aids. Based on your personality, you might find that you're naturally drawn towards one side of the equation or the other. It would behoove you to pay attention to both parts but, at a minimum, try to concentrate on the side of the equation that you believe is your weaker one.

Thus, if you're an objective thinker who is good with numbers, it's probably best to concentrate on the sections of the book that discuss how to quantify and qualify your emotions. Doing so will allow you to take a much more balanced approach to your *worth vs. worth it* decision. Vice versa for the *feelers* in the group, who are great with introspection, but don't believe that numbers are their strength. I truly keep the math in this book simple, since I'm not the brightest bulb myself!

The final chapter of this book (Chapter 14) is my financial philosophy viewed through the lens of the *Golden Albatross* decision-making process. Consider it a mix between a pep talk, a cautionary tale, and practical advice on how to apply all the tools this book arms you with. I originally crafted it as a speech to a class of mid-career officers at a service school who would soon hit their 10-year service mark. It's a traditional point where many U.S. military officers decide to leave military service. That speech, the blog post I turned it into, and the chapter it has now become, is by far my favorite piece of financial thought.

Following Chapter 14, I have placed a chronological Bibliography for every reference included in this book. I cite a lot of reference material throughout this book, and anywhere I reference another person's work I have provided a reference for you to follow up on. Doing so provides the authors the credit they deserve and proves to you that I'm not just making this stuff up. This brings up another good point regarding how to use this book, though. As you read it, you'll discover that I cite many of the same references over and over. Consider that my way of foot-stomping important points from the front of a classroom. I'm a big believer in repetition.

The Bibliography serves another purpose as well. I make a lot of pop culture references throughout the book to lighten the mood on what might otherwise be an extremely dreary topic. In fact, I make so many pop references that readers of the printed book stood to miss out if I didn't provide them a way to access the comic relief. Since the Bibliography lists the actual web address for the "cited" text from the body of the book, readers of the physical copy can type those addresses into their browser, if they so choose. I'll admit, this kills a bit of the spontaneity of my pop culture references, but at least people who like the tactile feel of a book can still participate in the fun...if only at three-quarters the speed of someone reading the e-book.

The bottom line is that this book offers a way to demystify a complex and personal decision that will impact you for the remainder of your life. No pressure there! But seriously, the decision to stick with, or leave, a pensionable job doesn't have to be made by running it through a black box of murky emotions and unquantified money considerations. There are ways to provide rigor and clarity to the decision. This book shows you my way.

Introduction

Despite the potentially dry subject matter of pensions and personal finance, I want you to know that I get personal in this book. I touch on some traditionally uncomfortable subjects related to our jobs, like physical hazard vs. monetary reward and mental health. I do that for a reason.

Not every job we do, profession we choose, or endeavor we undertake is worth the compensation we earn. Some jobs take a toll and it's not always obvious in the moment as to which jobs those are, or what that toll is. The long-term effects of a job or profession can sneak up if we don't maintain a conscious effort to monitor for them. If, all of a sudden, people wake up one day and think to themselves, *"this job demands far more of me than I am earning from it"* or *"I'm not sure I can last five more minutes, let alone five more years, no matter how big my pension,"* then they have a serious problem on their hands. Ideally, a person should intervene long before they reach that point, but that's not always possible.

The main method I choose to convey these complex issues is through stories. My stories range from the hilarious, to the scary, to the insane, to the heartbreaking, and everything in between. They include stories about me, my friends, my family, my co-workers, and most importantly, some of the readers of my blog. Most of the stories focus on how we grappled with issues centered around our jobs, monetary compensation, and the effect that had on us.

As a result, I've sanitized the names, locations, and personal information. I did this not only to protect those involved but because these job-related feelings are universal, so you don't need to know that "Joe" is my Cousin Arnold; that won't help you. What has helped many readers of GrumpusMaximus.com is getting down to the feelings that employees wouldn't otherwise mutter to their colleagues. It has been a major strength of the blog, and I hope it benefits you here, as well.

Other parts of this book are functional, and include visual aids, math formulas, and thought experiments. I use them to connect the personal stories to the practical techniques I have devised to determine if a pensionable job is worth staying at in the long run. No doubt, many readers will find the practical portions of this book more useful and easier to navigate.

However, since work is so much a part of personal identity, it's impossible to completely separate the emotions from the logic in a *Golden Albatross* decision. While some people prefer to think their way through problems, and other people prefer to feel their way through them, in reality, a person will need to do a lot of both for a decision as important as staying or leaving their pensionable job. Thus, for this book I've specifically captured content from my blog which, taken in its entirety, provides a holistic method for doing just that. I hope you find it useful.

Disclaimers and Definitions

A few disclaimers before we start. In no way do I consider myself, or should you consider me, a financial advisor or pension expert. Other than laboring for one myself, and writing a blog about pensions and Financial Independence (FI), I don't possess any official qualifications. I wrote this book to provide you information; information you should not take at face value. After reading this book you should either research your specific situation further or seek professional financial advice, preferably from a fee-only Certified Financial Planner™ (CFP). I find that fee-only CFPs have the least number of conflicts of interest within the financial advice industry. That said, I've grasped the potentially powerful role my pension could play in creating FI for me and my family. I also understand the potentially destructive role a dangling pension, so tantalizingly close, might play in one's calculation of happiness. That's why I'm sharing my knowledge with you.

Next, I'm not a spokesman for the United States military or government. That should be obvious since I'm writing under a pseudonym, but in case it's not, let me state clearly and plainly that the opinions expressed throughout this book are my own. They in no way reflect the policy of the Department of Defense (DoD) or my specific branch of the military—which, by the way, I don't disclose.

It's also worth noting that I assume some level of knowledge already in my readers. This saves time. Inside the confines of this book, you will only find definitions of potentially complicated financial topics as required by the flow and context of the chapters in which they are embedded. Yet, as I do in my blog posts, I reference or footnote to articles that describe and explain these basic foundational concepts for those who need them.

Finally, just as a point of clarification, throughout this book when I refer to a pension, I mean a Defined Benefit Pension (DBP) Plan. In other words, one where a person works an agreed amount of time for an organization and, based on a set formula, receives an amount of money paid until death as an annuity for that previous work. There are other types of pensions out there, but DBPs continue to serve as the standard, which is why I stick to that one definition.

THE GOLDEN ALBATROSS

PART ONE

Chapter 1

What is a Golden Albatross?

This Gets Worse Before It Gets Better

A *Golden Albatross* is a metaphor, and like all good metaphors, it begins with a story. In 2017, I reestablished communications with a friend of mine whom I had only spoken to sporadically over the previous decade. This friend is different from me in all the good ways I can think of: kind, full of empathy, and passionate about life. However, we are alike in many ways, too. As late adolescents and young adults, we both felt a calling to do something "greater" with our lives and chose a life of service. My friend chose to serve with humanitarian organizations to aid the neediest and most vulnerable children caught in wars around the world. I chose to serve in the U.S. military with the idea of protecting people like my friend. By the time we fell out of touch, we were well into our service-oriented careers with few regrets.

Fast forward a decade and my friend and I discovered we had a few more things in common. For one, we were disillusioned with our chosen callings and professions. Maybe it was inevitable that the scales of naivety would fall from our eyes at some point, dimming our faith in the virtue of our chosen paths. Yet, I found it a bit ironic that we reached those conclusions at almost the same time, especially considering how different and unconnected our lives had become over the intervening years. As we emailed and messaged each other about the events that led us to this point, we also discovered we had one other painful similarity in our stories—we both felt trapped by the tantalizing Defined Benefit Pension (DBP) connected to 20 years of service with our organizations.

For those of you who haven't heard of me before, and only know what you read about me in the preface, don't worry; I'll get into the gory details of my own painful decision to stick it out for 20 years in later chapters. In the meantime, trust me when I say that I put myself through great mental and emotional turmoil while determining if I could make it to that 20-year endpoint. It turned out that my friend was in a similar situation, but due to her circumstances, the difficulty of her decision was far greater than my own.

The Issue

My friend was sexually assaulted. She was assaulted while overseas delivering aid in a country devastated by civil war and genocide. As if that weren't bad enough, she was assaulted by her manager. That's right; while risking her life in a far-off war-torn country, where she very well could have been assaulted or killed by any number of armed combatants, the greatest threat turned out to be her boss.

Not unlike many women in her situation, my friend chose not to report what happened out of fear; fear for her safety, fear of retaliation, fear for her hard-won reputation, and fear for her career. Thus, she put up with his threats and harassment while continuing to work until the time came to leave that country.

Over the years, my friend dealt with the traumatic repercussions from the assault (on top of those caused by her fieldwork) as best as she could. She eventually found a job at her organization's headquarters.

This afforded her a break from the fieldwork, but again it put her in close working proximity to her assailant where, unfortunately, she also discovered his predatory behavior continued. Now more senior herself, she decided to report him. She was dealing with the emotional effects of this, a diagnosis of Post Traumatic Stress Disorder (PTSD), and burnout when we re-established contact.

My Reaction

Honestly, I didn't know what to say when my friend told me about all of this. While I had known from some of our intermittent communications over the years that she had experienced a mental breakdown, I didn't know the cause. When I found out, I went through a range of emotions from disbelief to rage.

My friend didn't want to feed my rage and she told me so. While I struggled to manage my own emotions and properly support her, my friend mentioned she felt trapped by the pension. She wanted to leave the organization at which she had spent 15+ years because it wasn't good for her mental health. She believed the organization fostered an environment that placed young idealistic women in vulnerable situations. Specifically, it placed women in situations where they were vulnerable to sexual abuse from their male colleagues. Her experience with reporting the assault only reinforced that belief. The organization's actions suggested it was only superficially committed to holding predators accountable.

As a result, my friend was at a major crossroads in life. That pension, so tantalizingly close with its lifetime of financial benefits, was nearly within reach. It seemed like a lot to simply throw away, especially after sacrificing so much. On the other hand, the job continued to cause documented damage to her mental health.

A Search for Meaning

I immediately latched on to this as a way to help, since I had just been through a similar experience. It so happened that I had written several pre-cursor blog posts in email form for co-workers on the topics of Financial Independence (FI) and pensions. I immediately sent them to her, and she got excited and enthusiastic. I also followed up with some tailored advice on how I made my *worth vs. worth it* decision.

As I helped my friend get smart on financial issues, FI, and the idea of creating a financial plan, we started throwing around the term *Golden Handcuffs* in reference to feeling trapped by our pensions. We thought that was the correct term. Thus, when my friend encouraged me to start a blog to help other people, I wanted to call the blog *Golden Handcuffs*. That is, until I Googled the term and found out that according to the almighty Wikipedia the term *Golden Handcuffs*:

> *...refers to financial allurements and benefits that have the objective to encourage highly compensated employees to remain within a company or organization instead of moving from company to company (or organization to organization).*

The key part is *highly compensated employee*, or, in other words, a business executive. Just for the record, that isn't me or my friend. Thus, I found myself in a conundrum.

I was stuck looking for a metaphor to describe a person's desire to leave their current job while feeling trapped by the need to hit their pension point. I did some research (i.e., I Googled for at least 30 seconds) and it turned out there wasn't one for that situation. Maybe back in the day when everyone had pensions it was just called "Life" or "Reality." Not these days though, when hardly anyone has a pension.

Golden Is Not Good

Undeterred, I started to crank out draft blog posts, and let the metaphor problem rest. Financially speaking, I had plenty to say and was in no hurry to address the issue. That was, until I wrote the post that would become Grumpus Maximus vs. the *Golden Albatross*. At that point, I had to come to grips with the need for a metaphor, as it proved central to the entire reason for starting my blog.

I started with the premise that the term had to include "Golden" as a reference to the rewards represented by the pension. Much like *Golden Handcuffs* though, the reward felt backhanded since it was trapping us. Given the disillusionment that developed over our careers, something which we previously felt so positive about, I started to think of metaphors associated with something once good, turning bad. Then I remembered the words of my favorite space captain, Mal Reynolds, from the movie *Serenity*...

Wait. What? You don't know *Serenity*? It was the sci-fi movie that came out the same year as *Star Wars Episode III*. No one went to see it, but trust me, it was one million times better than *Episode III*. It had the guy from the TV show *Castle* in case that rings any bells. Yes! That guy.

In the movie, Mal Reynolds (the *Castle* actor) is facing off with the bad guy (Academy Award® winner Chiwetel Ejiofor), who tells Mal that the girl he is trying to protect is "an Albatross." Mal corrects the bad guy by saying, "The way I remember it, is that the Albatross was a sign of good luck until some idiot killed it. Yes...I read a poem, try not to faint."

Of course, if you're anything like me, then we know from our Iron Maiden phase in life that the reference to "the poem" is *Rime of the Ancient Mariner* (which, admittedly, is not Iron Maiden's best song). Turns out that *Rime* was an actual poem before Iron Maiden made it infamous. Some guy named Samuel Taylor Coleridge wrote it— who knew?

Illustration: Rime of the Ancient Mariner

In any case, Mal had it right. The Albatross was good luck until the Mariner killed it with an arrow, bringing bad luck to his ship and crew. To atone to the fates/gods/spirits of the sea, his shipmates punished the Mariner by hanging the dead Albatross around his neck. Thus, the term "Albatross around the neck."

The metaphor crystallized in my mind. Our careers, once so bright and meaningful, now hung around our necks like the dead albatross. But, if we could suffer through the "punishment" (i.e., the last few years until vesting in our pension) that albatross would turn golden. The ultimate silver lining in our storm cloud. Damn it! I could have used that metaphor instead, but then the last part of this story would not be so good.

Damned Google

Thus, the *Golden Albatross* was born. Of course, I checked Google again. There I was with images of immortality in my head for coining a new metaphor only to find the number one result for *Golden Albatross* was a sexual act, as defined in Urban Dictionary.

Curse you, Internet gods, WHY MUST YOU MOCK ME!? I couldn't believe it. I mean Mrs. Grumpus and I like our "three minutes of ecstasy several times a month," but the Urban Dictionary definition is over the top. Undeterred, I scrolled further down the list of returns and noticed this link: The Rembrandts' "I'll Be There For You" was a *golden albatross*. I excitedly read the story and found this line buried within:

> *For a pair of musicians who had been making music...for the last five years as The Rembrandts, being known as the band associated with the Friends theme ended up being a "golden albatross," as Solem put it.*

Damn right! I think it's safe to say that *Friends* proved a *Golden Albatross* for everyone involved. Name one quality TV show or movie role that anyone from *Friends* has done since. David Schwimmer was by far the worst actor in *Band of Brothers*. Jennifer Aniston in *Office Space*? Maybe, but was that before or after *Friends* ended? In any case, I decided I was going to own the *Golden Albatross* term from that point forward, Urban Dictionary be damned.

Re-Cap

Now you know the story behind the *Golden Albatross*. To review, it's a metaphor I've coined to define the tension a person feels between the desire to leave their pensionable career on one hand, and the desire to stay for the pension on the other. The reasons for leaving don't have to be as bad as either mine or my friend's. However, being in a *Golden Albatross* situation sucks, no matter what the cause.

For some people, it sucks so bad that they either stay to the detriment of their health (or life), or they punch out. That's where both my friend and I found ourselves as we hit the latter part of our careers. I hope for your sake that's not you. Maybe the rest of this book can help you avoid such drama while making an educated and proactive decision at the same time? If not, and you're there now, then you've come to the right spot.

———

Interested in learning about the basics of a Defined Benefit Pension (DBP) plan or Golden Handcuffs? Check out the Chapter 1 resources at: https://grumpusmaximus.com/golden-albatross-book-chapter-resources/chapter-1/

Chapter 2
Worth vs. Worth It

My One No Shitter

In the branch of the military I served in, we have a tradition of telling truthful but over-the-top stories known as *No Shitters*. That designation is based on the reaction of your audience, which typically questions the veracity of said story with the colorful response of "No shit?" Alternatively, they might use "No bullshit?" Regardless, below is my one *No Shitter*. I've intentionally sanitized the events, locations, service branches, and names of participants to protect them and me from any potential fallout. If the story seems vague, that's why.

I know it's a lengthy story, but it's 100% germane to the topic of judging a thing's value and determining whether or not that value is worth the endeavor. In other words, it deals directly with the *Golden Albatross* conundrum, but colorfully, so stick with it. It's *worth it*. I promise.

The Believer

In late summer 2009, I almost killed myself while on a mission to interdict extremist-linked narcotics from the Afghanistan/Pakistan border area. At the time, I was in charge of a team of specialists that provided onsite support for larger units conducting counter-narcotics and other types of interdiction missions. It was a dream job that included the challenges of leadership, a lot of arduous training, and the potential to get out from behind the desk and *into the field*. This assignment embodied most of the reasons I joined the military and, at the time, I was a big believer in the importance of the missions we supported. I believed in it so much that I volunteered for that 2009 deployment, six-months after returning home from my first.

Our typical support package consisted of two technical specialists who would embed into larger units already deployed and working in an area where an interdiction was likely. These pairs of specialists were typically young E-4 through E-6s, which are the U.S. military's fourth through sixth lowest pay grades, usually 18 to 25 years old. Occasionally, my senior non-commissioned officer or I would work into the rotations to stagger the workload for our personnel. My senior non-com and I had the same training as our specialists, and I was big on leading from the front. We always had more missions than personnel, and by rotating-in, we provided them some rest and recuperation time at our base of operations.

My unit was a high-demand, low-density asset. I worked hard with our higher headquarters (HHQ) to assign my personnel to units with a high likelihood of requiring our skills based on their area of operations. Morale stayed high when real opportunities for work remained likely. Occasionally, the stars would align allowing us to embed personnel with a specific unit for a specific time based on a specific piece of intelligence. Everyone on the team liked these missions best. This is the type of mission I found myself supporting in the late summer of 2009.

On the day the order came down, a partially trained E-4 (who I'll call *Bob* for the rest of the story) and I were the only two non-embedded team members. Everyone else was already assigned. My HHQ made it clear that we would support the mission. Given my belief in the importance of the work we were doing, it wasn't like I was going to say "no" anyway. The only decision I had to make was whether I would take partially trained Bob with me.

What About Bob?

Bob was a great young man with a can-do attitude and a wickedly sharp mind. Strangely, he'd earned a college degree, then enlisted, rather than become an officer. It just so happened Bob and I came from the same home state. Only a few weeks prior, I had sent him home on compassionate leave to witness the birth of his first son.

Due to personnel rotations and timing, we didn't have the opportunity to get Bob fully trained before deployment. He had spent most of the deployment as our logistics, admin support, and "every other task we could think of guy." Up to that point, he'd stayed in the rear with me or my senior non-com. Motivation never flagging, his ability to accomplish anything we asked never ceased to amaze.

I still remember the pleading look he hit me with when the call came to support this mission. The one bit of training we'd given Bob before deployment was combat training. While he couldn't necessarily perform the specialist tasks of our unit, he could at least watch my six and provide a second set of hands and eyes on target.

What could possibly go wrong with this scenario? In my mind, there was nothing so bad that would prevent me from taking him. So, I did.

Things Go Sideways

Of course, things went wrong. All sorts of wrong. We linked up with the unit we'd be working with, conducted some training and weapons qualifications, and then waited for the intelligence to tip us off. The morning of the mission we rolled-up on the target at first light, immediately detained the traffickers and began searching for their narcotics. We knew from previous experience the narcotics would likely be well-hidden somewhere on the target. It took us eight hours in the blazing late-summer sun, but the team finally found them. All in all, we approximated we'd found one to two tons of hash. There may have been opium, too, but we never got the chance for a closer examination.

By the time we found the narcotics, the scene had turned somewhat chaotic. Throughout our eight-hour search, we had discovered enough circumstantial evidence that the unit commander (whom I'll call Phil) felt compelled to stay on target. Phil's HHQ, who of course was not on the scene, grew more nervous as time ticked on without a major narcotics find. HHQ started placing more pressure on Phil to pull the unit out. Our mission was drawing a lot of attention from civilians in the area, any number of which could have turned into opposition forces (OPFOR).

By this point, the traffickers, who had protested their innocence all day, had started to agitate as well. In a moment of self-doubt, decision fatigue, and/or in an attempt to placate his HHQ to buy a few more minutes on target, Phil decided to loosen the traffickers' bonds and allow them to have a smoke. It proved an ill-timed decision, made only moments before we discovered the main haul of narcotics. Although I outranked Phil and didn't agree with the decision, I backed it because it wasn't my unit so it wasn't my call. All I could do was tell Bob to zip his body armor up extra tight and "be ready for anything."

Whether by a prearranged signal or simply seizing a moment of inattentiveness caused by the discovery of the narcotics, one of the traffickers bolted for an entryway into a structure located next to the narcotics. At this point, all hell broke loose. Several unit members, plus Bob, chased the trafficker into this structure which we'd cleared numerous times throughout the day. Most of the other traffickers used that commotion to disperse like a murder of crows, with unit members chasing after them. It was literally like some awful version of Keystone Kops, but with the U.S. military starring as the cops.

I had barely pulled my attention away from the hash I was examining in time to see Bob disappear into the structure. At that point, time slowed to a crawl and a gaping pit opened in my stomach. Researchers may have discovered scientific evidence for the time-warping effect that people perceive in circumstances like this. The leading theory posits that the brain records life-threatening events in such rich detail that upon replay it takes the brain that much longer to work through all the extra data. Whatever the cause, I can attest it's real. I can also attest that as I typed this part of the story, my body experienced several of the physiological reactions I felt in that moment, ten long years ago.

Before I could do or say anything, I heard loud and authoritative shouting coming from the direction of a cooking area on the side of the aforementioned structure. One of the traffickers had tipped over the kerosene used for cooking and was about to flick his cigarette into it. A unit member, with his hand on his holstered sidearm, was yelling at the trafficker to put the cigarette down. No one was quick enough on the draw. The gas, the structure, and the drugs went up in flames like some hokey Hollywood movie.

Did I say the traffickers scattered earlier? Well, now it was our turn. Everyone in the unit started to bug out. I dare not say "retreat," but they sure as hell ran away bravely while falling back to a safe rally point. Everyone except for me.

Don't get me wrong. I wasn't rooted in place based on some noble idea of standing my ground in the face of our now revealed enemy. Nope, I was transfixed by this singular thought as I watched the fire engulf the entryway through which I had last seen Bob disappear:

Shit! I'm going to have to go in there. I'll be damned if I'm going to come back without this brand-new father's ass in tow.

Some people might think that was brave, but don't confuse bravery with guilt. I was the one who had brought half-trained Bob on the mission, ordered him "to be ready for anything," and then lost track of him while I examined the narcotics. He was my responsibility that day and I had failed. My only thought was to try to rectify that situation.

I would love to say I calmly moved towards the flames, booming out his name like some sort of parade ground drill instructor. In reality, I was probably shrieking his name with tears streaming down my face like a toddler crying for his mama after a skinned knee. Fortunately, just before I hit the smoke-filled entryway, I heard a familiar voice shouting my name. I turned back to look...and there was Bob already at the rally point!

I was too relieved at seeing Bob's shiny face to be pissed-off at the fact that he'd left his fearless leader on target. Praising every deity I could name under that now smoke-filled sun, I took that as my cue and got the hell out of there. Yes, my only combat-like story ends with a retreat in the face of arson, but without a single shot fired. If I could figure out some way of embedding the song *Brave, Brave, Sir Robin* from the movie *Monty Python and the Holy Grail* into this book, I would do so at this point.

Aftermath

Oddly enough, while I remember so vividly the minutiae leading up to the fire, my memory fails me on some of the details from the aftermath. Once we were safe, Bob told me how he'd chased his trafficker into the structure. He and several of the unit members restrained the guy as he attempted to set fire to it from the inside. I can't remember if they evacuated through another entry/exit point (there were two), or if they exited from the same point they'd entered and I just lost track of them in the commotion. Either way, I would have charged into an empty flaming space with a good chance of succumbing to the smoke.

What about the traffickers? They got away. I guess they'd calculated that without the evidence, U.S. forces wouldn't do anything to them. They were right. Hopefully, some pissed-off Afghan or Pakistani warlord took care of them for setting fire to his product, but it's unlikely. Those countries are so awash with narcotics that the loss of this particular stash probably didn't even dent the bottom line.

Phil's unit made a weak attempt to go after the traffickers in the moments immediately following our displacement from the target. Civilian interference quickly put an end to the effort though. Shortly after that, Phil's HHQ ordered us to evacuate to their location, despite what those of us on-scene felt to be an obvious act of aggression. If I had to guess, HHQ calculated with the narcotics destroyed, none of their personnel injured, and a dicey on-scene situation developing, there was no need to press their luck. *C'est la Guerre!*

Worth vs. *Worth It*

As I stated at the beginning of this chapter, some of you may be wondering why I bothered to relate this exciting, somewhat unbelievable, and mostly off-topic story in a book about pensions and FI. Fair enough. I did so because I believe it illustrates the complexities of answering any *worth vs. worth it* equation, where the value of something is definable on one hand, but the effort exerted to achieve that something is not. I see the following questions a lot in the FI forums and Facebook pages I engage on: "What is my pension worth?"

and "Is my pension worth it?" One is a straightforward question of value. The other is as subjective and dependent on individual circumstances as they come.

Let's examine a few of the points within my story and, hopefully, you'll see what I mean. I'll start with the narcotics. The narcotics that burned up in that lovely fireball most definitely held a certain amount of worth or street value. Had the traffickers not destroyed them, we could have calculated that worth based on their weight and composition. For argument's sake, let's say there was only hash within that haul of drugs, and it totaled $5 million in street value. "That's a lot of monies!"

Yet, was it *worth it*? Was interdicting $5 million of illegal narcotics worth almost dying? Was it worth Bob almost dying? Was it worth that hollow feeling of *expendability* I still get every time I think about those tragi-comedic events while shaving in the morning? I argue *absolutely not*.

I base that answer on an insight I alluded to earlier. Afghanistan and Pakistan are so awash in narcotics, the destroyed ones probably failed to register as a blip on some warlord's bottom line. If you multiplied that day's efforts by 100 it still wouldn't have made an ounce of difference to U.S. wartime objectives. Had someone died, their sacrifice would have amounted to something akin to pissing on a forest fire. I doubt the Department of Defense would have worded their posthumous award citation in that manner, but the futility of our effort remains stubbornly lodged in my mind.

Another good example of a *worth vs. worth it* calculation is the one I made when I believed Bob was trapped in a burning structure. Whether I made the decision consciously or subconsciously, out of guilt or for some other reason, I calculated the value of Bob's life as equal to my own. So, for me, the answer to the question of whether it was *worth it* to run into that flaming structure to save Bob was *yes*.

As a quick, therapeutic segue, I don't type those words or thoughts lightly. In the intervening years, I spent so much time dwelling on my negative feelings from that day that I never stopped to examine anything positive I might have learned about myself. Certainly, I'm happy we survived. Every time I get an email or the opportunity to catch up with Bob, I know things turned out for the best. But like a dog with a bone, I've never been able to let those negative feelings go. Maybe writing all of this down will help. I never said all of the lessons learned from this story would be financial.

Postscript for Future Pensioners

There remains one final way in which this episode touches upon a *worth vs. worth it* calculation. It might be the most germane reason to my readers, especially those who stand to earn a pension while working potentially thankless jobs. If you couldn't tell, the events I relate in this story played a role in my 2016 mental breakdown. It wasn't the primary cause, but it was a contributing factor. After my breakdown, I was unsure if I could finish out three more years in the military and earn my pension. It proved to be a *worth vs. worth it* decision. Was the more than $1 million I would earn from a military pension worth the potential long-term damage I might do to my mental health if I served three more years? It was my *Golden Albatross* moment and ultimately, I decided yes it was *worth it*.

Of course, I made that *Golden Albatross* decision based on my situation and factors, several of which I will address in Chapter 3. However, let me preface them now and say those may not be your factors or any other person's factors. This probably means that I can't directly help you when it comes time to determine if your specific pension is *worth it*; much like you couldn't have helped me decide if running into that burning structure was *worth it*. Those types of decisions are just too personal. However, I hope my *No Shitter* will at least allow you to frame those types of decisions better, if and when it comes time to do so.

With that said, I can show you how to bin your feelings and emotions about your job on one side of the *worth vs. worth it* equation. I can also show you how to calculate what your pension is worth on the other—just like I could have calculated the value of those narcotics had the traffickers not destroyed them. I calculated my pension's worth during my *Golden Albatross* moment, and I've helped others calculate theirs since starting my blog. I intend to show you how throughout the remainder of this book.

One final plea, which I'll make several times throughout this book. If you feel trapped in your own *Golden Albatross* situation and are suffering mental health issues, it's okay to seek help. You're not weak for doing so but strong for taking action. Utilize those mental health resources from the medical coverage that your pensionable job (hopefully) provides. That's why they're there. A lot of pension-earning jobs suck or have long periods that suck. They will impact you for the rest of your life. That's why our employers dangle a pension at the end of it, to make us stay despite *the suck*. You don't have to suffer alone, though.

Interested in learning more about worth vs. worth it decision making?
Or, would you rather look at some pictures of the narcotics from my story?
Either way check out the Chapter 2 resources at: https://grumpusmaximus.com/golden-albatross-book-chapter-resources/chapter-2/

Chapter 3
Why Would One Stay?

To Stay or Go? That is a Question

As I mentioned at the end of Chapter 2, the *worth vs. worth it* nature of the *Golden Albatross* inflection point implies a decision. Like The Clash song, *Should I Stay Or Should I Go*, you're deciding to stay or go. Unlike the song, just because you go, it doesn't mean trouble. And, if you stay it doesn't necessarily mean double. But, you need some good reasons for either staying or going. So, in this chapter, I'm going to address some of the reasons I stayed. I will specifically address why and how I decided to stay at my pensionable job in the military. This will act as a foil to Chapter 5, where I discuss what I consider to be some valid reasons for leaving a pensionable career.

Now, you might be thinking, "isn't it obvious, Grumpus? A person stays for the money." Like Academy Award® winner Cuba Gooding, Jr. in the movie *Jerry McGuire*, you may even be shouting "Show me the money!" right now, to which I would answer both "yes" and "no."

Certainly, if you choose to stay for the pension, you are staying for the money. Yet, money is just a tool, not an end state. If you stay for the money, you're staying because the money can do something, or several things, for you. This means the first question you need to answer, before deciding if a pension is *worth it*, is what can that pension do for you.

Illustration: Show me the money.

That's No Easy Task

You're damn right, it's not an easy task. Let me share another story with you to prove my point. I already mentioned my 2016 mental breakdown several times, and I promise that I will address the main driver for that breakdown in Chapter 6, so hang in there. What I haven't mentioned up to this point, though, is that in conjunction with that breakdown I also went through an anxiety-fueled Mid-Life Crisis (MLC). I'll try to recreate the scene for you if I can.

There I was in spring 2016, with 17 years in the military, actively melting down on several mental fronts. I was angry, depressed, and highly agitated. It physically felt like the *Golden Albatross* had been hung around my neck. I wasn't sure if I could make it another day, let alone three more years in the military. But it also felt like I couldn't simply quit, forgo all those retirement benefits, and start a new career with two kids and a wife depending on me. I believed my only option was to tough it out until my 20-year point.

But then what? I assumed the pay from a 20-year pension wouldn't be enough to cover my family's post-military retirement expenses. I believed that I would need to start a second career, ideally as far away from the military as possible. What would that career be though? Was it even realistic to expect that I could start an entirely different career in my mid-40s?

I had all these feelings, beliefs, assumptions, and questions but no solid answers and no way to test them. This post-military career-linked anxiety was part of what drove me crazy. It led to a MLC centered on the question of what I would do if/when I chose to leave the military. This was an existential crisis and I was an absolute mental mess.

"It's Merely a Flesh Wound"

Wow. Seeing all of my issues spelled out in words makes them sound insurmountable. They weren't. I'm thankful I didn't punch any work colleagues, cheat on my wife, or buy a red sports car. And, while I didn't drink myself into stupors, stop showing up for work, or contemplate suicide, I was deeply unhappy and angry. Worse, it started to impact my family, which was one of the reasons I ultimately sought help.

Thanks to therapy, a mild amount of medication, hard work, and a lot of introspection I got the upper hand on my PTS-linked depression. However, my PTS-linked anxiety required a more unique solution. Fortunately, I stumbled across that solution during what I erroneously believed was an unrelated journey to increase my financial literacy. When I realized the implications of what I discovered though, it solved a large portion of my anxiety almost overnight.

The Answer to All of My Problems?

What was the answer? Simple, it was Financial Independence (FI). That's a term I've thrown around a few times now, so let me define it for you. FI means you have enough financial assets to meet all your needs without the fear of running out of money or needing to work again.

I didn't make that up. People far smarter than I am created that term. I only grasped its true implication when I heard blogger and author JL Collins interviewed about his book *The Simple Path to Wealth* on the Mad Fientist podcast during the immediate aftermath of my breakdown. When I did, I rushed to download the book and consumed it in one night. That led me to several other books and blogs like Darrow Kirkpatrick and Chris Mamula's *Can I Retire Yet?* As I did this, I realized three things:

1. My 20-year military pension could be a potentially powerful FI tool that would cover a lot, but not all, of my family's post-military retirement spending.

2. From that point forward, if Mrs. Grumpus and I invested the savings we had already amassed correctly, along with any future savings, we could conceivably build a big enough nest egg to cover the "gap" between what my pension would pay and what our projected post-military retirement expenses would be.

   ■ Most importantly, we could do this with a high probability that our nest egg would never run out.

3. If successful, I could truly retire (i.e. never work again) if I so chose. Therefore, I didn't need to worry about what I would do next!

Retiring early by achieving FI is known as FIRE (Financially Independent Retire Early). No words can appropriately describe the feeling of relief that my FIRE realization provided me. It was then, and remains now, a powerful piece of knowledge.

Pensions Can Be Powerful FI Tools, But Savings Can Too

Are you wondering how I planned to accumulate enough wealth in only three short years to overcome the need to ever work again? The answer to that question wasn't because my forthcoming military pension would be so big that my family would never need to rely on investments or savings. Even with the generous benefits provided by a military pension, my projections showed that the pension would only cover two-thirds of my family's annual expenses. Maybe back in the 1950s through the 1970s a person could work a job for 20 to 30 years, not save a penny, and still expect to live comfortably off their

DBP. However, these days pensions of any sort in the U.S. are a rare thing, let alone *BIG* pensions. So, I knew my family and I would need savings and investments.

Fortunately, though, and without any real intention, I had already placed my family on a path to FI by 2016. I was always a good saver when single, and when Mrs. Grumpus and I married, we became good savers together—although not without difficulty. We also proved to be at least mediocre investors, which helped. Of course, we got financially lucky at a few points along the way too, which didn't hurt.

That isn't to say we didn't make financial mistakes as a couple. We made several large ones including the purchase of a condominium in San Diego in 2004 at the height of the Southern California housing bubble. In doing so, we committed a significant amount of money, previously invested in a basket of stocks, as the down payment. While it meant the mortgage was never worth more than the condo (aka: we were never underwater), even during the 2008-2009 Great Recession, it also meant that we missed out on all the gains those stocks would have amassed from 2004 until 2019 (when we eventually sold the condo).

Whereas our "investment" in the condo managed returns in the low single digits, the gains on that basket of stocks would have crushed it by multiples of ten. We literally would have been millionaires, but that misses the point. Had we kept the stocks, not bought the condo, and ended up millionaires, the independence that money could have provided might have changed the calculation during my *Golden Albatross* moment.

Of course, that's a lot of "would haves" and "could haves," and one big "might have." In reality, the money from those stocks wasn't there and my *Golden Albatross* moment happened along with my MLC. That said, a large savings rate covers for a lot of financial mistakes, and my wife and I had trained ourselves to save anywhere between 20% to 30% of our annual income. This meant we could absorb the occasional large misstep, even one as big as the condo.

Disciplining ourselves to save created an additional advantage on our path to FI; it made us accustomed to living on less. That lifestyle choice paid large dividends when I calculated our projected post-military retirement budget. Because we had learned to live on less, our projected post-retirement budget appeared modest as I ran the numbers. Upon that discovery, I realized we wouldn't need a nest egg much larger than what we already saved. Thus, the goal of creating a nest egg big enough to cover *the gap* between what my pension would pay, and what our annual budget required, would be that much easier to achieve.

As a result, I was able to calculate that the three years between my mental breakdown and my 20-year retirement date was all we needed to put us *over the top* with our savings. But...it had to be a conscious decision. While it wouldn't require that much extra sacrifice, it would require intentionality in our money decisions. Most importantly, the savings and budgeting only worked in conjunction with the pension. The key to all of this remained my pending military-provided DBP.

The Path to FI-lightenment

After I realized all of this, it only took me a few weeks to create a financial plan and test it using a high-powered retirement calculator. Those tests showed me that my plan had a high probability of success. Therefore, it's important to note that I didn't simply dream about FI. I created a plan, wrote it down, thoroughly stress-tested it, and modified it as necessary. Nor did I stop at just one round of planning and testing. Every time I updated my plan, I subjected it to new tests. So far, my plan has gone through several iterations brought about by life's randomness. This includes a change of intended retirement location from San Diego to New Zealand; a change in homeownership expectations from immediately buying a forever home to renting for the first several years; and various changes in how we intend to fund university for our two kids.

For now, the plan endures, but of course, the real test will only come after the first few years of retirement when I can check our actual expenditures against my proposed budget. That said, I'm not overly concerned about the money, given how thoroughly I've planned for retirement. As a result, I'm able to manage most of my retirement anxiety with the knowledge that my past and current sacrifices provide the basis for my family's future financial stability. Not only that, but knowing that the pension provides an income floor beneath which my family will never fall also helps with managing the anxiety.

My Why

As I said at the beginning of this chapter, the decision to stay or leave a pensionable job is about more than just the money. Part of the decision is about what you think the pension money could do for you *if you stayed*. For me, it was specifically about what the pension could do in conjunction with the other money my wife and I had saved and invested. My goal was to FIRE when I retired, but I needed both the pension and my savings/investments to do that. That successful combination will allow me and my wife to live the remainder of our lives knowing that we'll never need to work *just for the money* again.

I'm not saying we'll never work again. If we move to New Zealand, then one of us will need to work for a few years in order to obtain a permanent resident visa for the family. However, the choices of where to work, who to work for, and how little we're willing to be paid, will be just that: our choice and not anyone else's. For instance, if my wife or

I wanted to go to work for a non-profit with low pay but a mission to make the world a better place, we could do that.

The sweet kicker is that my wife and I will be able to do all of this while providing a great life for our kids. This knowledge provides me a large part of the peace of mind I need to function at work and home, in spite of the breakdown. This also made my final years in the military a lot more bearable.

What's Your Why?

That's my reason for staying, but it isn't necessarily your reason. We all have our motivations, needs, and wants in life. Don't get me wrong—if a lightbulb clicked on in your head as I explained why I stayed for my pension, that's great! Write me an email and let me know. Notes like that help to keep my fragile ego inflated...er ...ummm...I mean I *love* knowing that I helped people.

Seriously though, achieving FI or FIRE may not be your reason for staying. No biggie if that's the case. But if not, what is? Is it travel? More family time? Do you want to watch your grandkids grow up without having to worry about income later in life? I know a guy who completely scrapped his easy living retirement plan, and decided to use the security of his pension income to assist his daughter with taking care of her husband (his son-in-law) who was tragically left wheelchair bound after a horrible car accident.

Now, I'm not saying your reason needs to be as noble as that guy's, but it should be just as clear. I say that as someone who hit year 17 out of 20 in a pensionable career field and seriously considered walking away from it. I found a reason to stay, which was about more than just the money, but I had to endure an awful experience to get to my why. Tough times may head your way, too. I hope not, but they may. If they do, you need to understand what would motivate you to stay and help you see out those tough times.

If you can't do that, then you won't be able to make an effective *worth vs. worth it* decision. In fact, it may be an indicator that you should go, not stay. I'll cover reasons to leave a pensionable job in Chapter 5. In the meantime, let's take the lessons learned from this chapter and use them to better inform the discussion in the next chapter on *Gutting It Out.*

Interested in more Financial Independence (FI) information?
Check out the Chapter 3 resources at: https://grumpusmaximus.com/golden-albatross-book-chapter-resources/chapter-3/

Chapter 4

Gutting It Out

Job Dissatisfaction

Sooooo...you're unhappy with your current job, eh? Not getting the sense of satisfaction that you once did? Or, maybe, you never felt like that at all? Maybe every day feels like a slog? No matter what, something drew you to contemplate leaving your pensionable career. Well, I got news for ya, pal. It turns out you're not alone; a lot of people do. In fact, according to a Gallup poll conducted in 2017, only 33% of American workers were actively engaged at work.

Many of those disengaged workers hated their jobs. If you hate your job, any length of time until retirement seems like a long time. Fortunately, if that's you, just search *"what to do if you hate your job"* and you'll find an endless number of articles and videos to help you. Sources range from major news sites to personal finance blogs and mental health websites.

It also turns out that for a fairly large percentage of folks, job satisfaction maps out as a U-shaped curve throughout their career. That means a lot of people start with high job satisfaction, but as they move towards the middle span of their career their satisfaction drops until it hits bottom. From that point onward satisfaction rebounds and continues to improve until retirement. The job satisfaction U-shape appears to parallel people's satisfaction with life. Much like I just described above, many people start with a lot of life satisfaction in their early adult lives, only to see it bottom out in their 40s. It then rebounds and recovers from their 50s onward. I drew a picture for you below that models this finding.

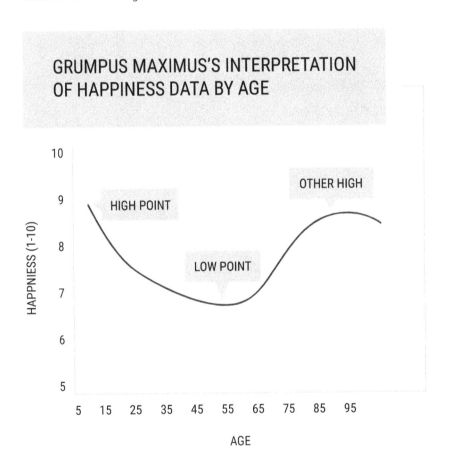

Figure 1: It Looks Like a Creepy Clown Smile!

Now, the difference in your case is that you're contemplating doing something about your job or career dissatisfaction. For whatever reason, you want to make a move. However, unlike most modern workers in today's economy, you have access to a DBP. What's more, the thought of walking away from that pension is holding you back. Maybe, as discussed in Chapter 3, you have a great reason for sticking around for the pension. Thus, taking everything above into account, the easiest approach may be determining whether or not quitting your job is going to fix your problem.

This is important because, as I pointed out above, you may be on the bottom end of that U-curve in life and your career. Changing jobs in such a case won't fix the problem. I would hate for you to embark on the effort-filled mental journey that the *Golden Albatross* decision cycle requires only to realize that the issue isn't the job, but you. An even worse result would be working your way through the entire *worth vs. worth it* equation, concluding that the pension is not worth it, quitting your job, but then realizing that the job wasn't the problem.

Let's Start with the Subjective

As a result of the science behind the job dissatisfaction problem, and to avoid major career and retirement blunders, I've decided to start with the subjective side of the *worth vs. worth it* equation. Doing so will force you to come to grips with what exactly troubles you about your current position. If that makes you uncomfortable, don't panic, because I, too, would prefer to jump in and start crunching numbers right away in the pursuit of an empirical answer to the problem.

However, as you are going to discover, there are no pure empirical answers to the *Golden Albatross* decision. There's just as much subjective weighting of mental and emotional issues as there are calculations on the Future Value (FV) of your pension. Besides, getting out of our comfort zone is good for all of us. It forces us to examine problems and issues in ways that we might not otherwise.

Not only that, but by working through the subjective issues first, you may realize you don't need to go further in the *Golden Albatross* decision process. You may realize that with a few tweaks, or a lifestyle change, the situation is tolerable. Or, at least tolerable enough to make it through to the pension—which brings us to the topic of *gutting it out*.

Not a No Shitter, But True, Nonetheless

A while back, I was soliciting ideas for blog articles in the Financial Independence (FI) for pensioners Facebook group that I run called *Golden Albatross*/Golden Handcuffs. I floated the idea of *Coping Strategies for the Last Few Years (i.e., Gutting It Out)* and received the following response from one of my group members:

> *"I have 6 years. Help me gut it out, and keep my eyes on the prize."*

Six years, eh? That's probably not an all-too-uncommon timeframe for this feeling to surface. I find that pension earners start to feel trapped near the end of their career when retirement (with a pension and the freedom it represents) feels so close, but yet so far.

It's important to note that, in this context, I don't consider feeling trapped as the same feeling as the *Golden Albatross*. I define the *Golden Albatross* as the tension a person feels between staying and leaving a pensionable career. In contrast, the trapped feeling surfaces *after* a person decides to stay and earn the pension, but *before* that person can retire with the pension's full benefits. That's the point where I find that *gutting it out* truly comes into play.

That said, I think coping strategies are 100% worth engaging in before making a *Golden Albatross* decision, which is why I've decided to devote an entire chapter to them in this book. Stepping through some of these coping strategies may not only help alleviate the symptoms of job dissatisfaction but may also help you identify the root problem.

Caveats and Qualifications

Much like I did earlier in the book regarding my financial qualifications, I feel compelled to state my (lack of) medical qualifications for the record. I'm not a medical doctor. More importantly, please remember that I suffered a mental breakdown due to work-related psychological trauma. Although I'm in recovery, I'm not recovered. This means I'm still very much a work in progress.

As I outline some of the coping strategies that helped me gut out my last few years in the military, there's no guarantee they'll work for anyone else. Thus, use discretion as you read this chapter. If your problems feel out of control, do your research and make sure you talk with a medical professional. There's no shame in it.

Secondly, despite not being a medical professional, I feel it's safe to say that for some people *gutting it out* isn't healthy or the right choice. While engaging in situations outside a person's comfort zone may be good for building resiliency, day-in and day-out engagement with a stressful situation wears and tears on a person's body and psyche. Some situations may be too toxic or harmful to be *worth it*.

That isn't to say that all people approaching the end of their career feel trapped. Some people like Warren Buffet and Charlie Munger truly love their jobs, and can't imagine a life without them. They'll never quit.

However, that's probably not you. Otherwise, why would you be reading this book? So, take everything I recommend with a grain of salt. Set up some guard rails to ensure that things don't get worse instead of better. Check on your assumptions from time to time and see if anything changed. In other words, use common sense when utilizing the following coping strategies.

Coping Strategy #1: Make a Plan

One day, a nurse at the Pain Management clinic I attend said something worth noting. She said, "A goal not written down is just a wish." It caught my attention because it was similar to a quote by Antoine de Saint-Exupéry that I am familiar with, "A goal without a plan is just a wish."

I agree, and that should come as no surprise since there's an entire section of my blog dedicated to financial planning. The reason I dedicate so much time to planning is that I find power in the written word.

Now obviously I'm not the first to coin the phrase "power in the written word" or to discover the effect, even in the financial world. Search for the phrases "the power of the written word" or "the power of the written plan" on the Internet and no shortage of material will appear.

However, as I just described in Chapter 3, I cannot emphasize enough the positive emotional and psychological effect that simply drafting and testing my retirement plan created. It helped me feel in control of many circumstances in my life that previously felt out of control. It's probably the closest thing I've ever felt to a religious experience outside of learning to surf!

It turns out that it's not just a feeling. Something physiologically transformative happens when a person takes time to write a plan. As Mary Morrissey pointed out on Huffington Post, when a person writes a plan it forces the logical hemisphere of the brain to translate the goal (up to that point merely an idea) from the creative hemisphere of the brain. That cross-over act happens in the corpus callosum, which is a bunch of neural fibers connecting the two hemispheres. When that occurs, electrical currents are shot down through the spine into every nerve ending of your body. As Mary put it:

> ...you send your consciousness and every cell of your body a signal that says, "I want this, and I mean it!"

There's another important effect: writing a plan down tremendously increases the odds of success for achieving your goals. That could prove pivotal if you find yourself lacking motivation and/or feeling trapped in your current work environment.

Who knows? You may even spot an opportunity to change or improve your circumstances once you write that plan. If you don't know how to write a retirement plan, check out the resources link at the end of this chapter.

Coping Strategy #2: Change Your Circumstances

One of the virtues of serving in the military (depending on your service and specialty) is that you change locations and job responsibilities a lot. As I reflected at the end of my career, I realized that occurred routinely every two-to-three years for me. None of those changes were small. Every single one involved moving from one side of the country to the other, if not overseas. They also involved a change in work duties and responsibilities. As a result, things rarely got stale. Just about the time a job transitioned from routine to boring, it was time to move again.

Of course, that has its downsides, too. Moving every two to three years is hard on the family. It's also tiresome. At some point, you yearn for a place to put down roots and call home. However, I'm not implying that everyone should move or change jobs as frequently as I have. What I'm saying is if you feel trapped in your job, or bored, or unmotivated, maybe it's time for a change.

That change need not be a move away from whatever company or organization you're currently working for, either. If you're getting long in the tooth, I would discourage a move if your pension is at stake. What I would recommend is you look for new or different opportunities within your current company or organization.

Maybe that's a lateral move to a different department, or maybe it's a reduction in responsibilities if you're getting too stressed. It could mean a move within the same company or organization but to an entirely different locale. Whatever the case, maybe your lack of motivation or the entrapment you're feeling is more about a perceived lack of control in your life and less about the job itself. If that's the case, stop letting your work-life simply happen to you and look for a way to take back some control.

Coping Strategy #3: Take More Time Off

Here's a scary quote from The Economist about unused paid vacation days:

> In effect, many Americans spend part of the year working for nothing, donating the equivalent of $561 on average to their firms.

That's a lot of beer! Project Time Off reports that 52% of Americans leave earned vacation days unused at the end of the year. While that's a downward trending statistic over the last three years, it's still above historical norms. This means that if you're an American, there's a one-in-two chance that you're guilty of subsidizing your organization.

Use your vacation time, people. It's good for you! Americans have a habit of looking down their noses at other nations, especially European ones, who vacation for entire months at a time. I don't! Or at least I no longer do. I want more of it, and so should you!

Time off needs not translate to an expensive vacation. The closer you get to retirement the more you may want to consider taking time off specifically to practice your intended retirement routine. Fritz Gilbert, from the Retirement Manifesto blog, did exactly that in 2017. He wrote a great article chronicling his lessons learned from his retirement dry run. I found his advice to avoid obligations during mini-retirement and to take time for contemplating full retirement the most useful.

As for me, after my mental breakdown I made sure to take all of my earned leave each year. That lifestyle alteration was made easier by a Department of Defense (DoD) rule change a few years ago which lessened the number of leave days active duty service members could carry over from one year to the next. Regardless, I stopped looking at my large number of saved up leave days as a good thing, and took my days even if I wasn't taking a major vacation. Even if I'm not taking a major vacation, I still take my days. It does me good.

Coping Strategy #4: Do More Stuff Outside of Work

Here's another thing that I came to appreciate after my breakdown: at some point, the career will end, but life will go on. Make sure you have a life worth living waiting for you on the other side. That's going to mean a lot of different things to different people. For me, a father with young kids and a wife, that meant family. My family was the motivating factor that led me to seek medical help after my breakdown. I wanted to ensure I had a wife and children who loved me and wanted to be with me once it was time to *pop smoke*, as we say in the military.

However, it also came to mean other things as well. Over my career, there were important and meaningful friendships in my life I allowed to atrophy—all because I was *too busy* with work. I've subsequently made meaningful strides to re-establish connections with some of those friends. On a different front, there was a creative calling within me that needed unleashing—which explains this book and the blog. Do you have some creative force ready to unleash on the world?

Finally, I had a deep desire to recapture some of my previous physical fitness. This not only meant getting to the doctor for a diagnosis on all my various physical ailments, but more time spent exercising. Thus, I started karate lessons with Grumpus Minimus #1, started biking to/from work (with all its associated mishaps), and started hiking more with my family.

So, what activities outside of work motivate you? Hobbies? Friends? Family? Whatever they are, I suggest you take some time away from work to start refining and expanding those activities into something more meaningful. Not only will it help you get through the day-to-day grind, but it will also set you up nicely for what comes next in your life after the career. Who knows? Your workdays may start to fly as you wake up each morning filled with anticipation for what you will do after work is done.

Coping Strategy #5: Limit Your Vices

I was going to call this coping strategy *Focus on the Positive*, but let's be honest; with a pseudonym like Grumpus Maximus it would be a bit disingenuous. To be fair, I'm the last person who should preach about limiting vices, since I struggle with my own routinely. My personal favorite is beer. I love good beer and drink too much of it. I shouldn't, though, because it aggravates both my mental and physical ailments. However, most nights I'll savor one or two to relax.

Fortunately, my body developed an internal defense mechanism a few years back in the form of an instant headache. That's right! My body doesn't wait to manifest a hangover the following morning. Instead, I get one instantly. It happens if I drink more than three beers in a night. This means that, fortunately, I'm forced to moderate.

Not everyone is as lucky. Before I retired, a senior non-commissioned officer (SNCO) I worked with reminded me of that fact. He'd been in the service for about as long as I had but had suffered far more psychologically, including combat-related mental health issues and the death of a spouse. He was also a recovering alcoholic and a single father.

Unfortunately, this SNCO suffered an alcohol relapse and barely escaped getting booted from the service. This was a person who had sat for hours in my office discussing FI, investing, the power of the pension, and his post-military plans. In other words, he knew the stakes, but his injuries and illness almost got the best of him. I'm happy to say my command was willing to give him another chance, and so was I. However, he's now walking a tightrope, and unlike me, he's still several years from retirement.

Thus, make no mistake; if you're *gutting it out* at work, you're in a vulnerable mental place. Those vices can sneak up quickly when you're not looking. The next thing you know, they've got control of you. That's about the time you do something stupid. Maybe it's drinking and driving, or maybe it's punching your boss. Either way, you need a method for maintaining control of those negative and self-destructive urges. Now, I'm not saying you should become a teetotaler or a Buddhist monk. What I am saying is that you should take all things in moderation and *focus on the positive*.

Conclusion

Arriving at a point in your career where you feel the need to *gut it out*, especially for the pension, is stressful. I know because I was on the tail end of it not too long ago. However, you need not resign yourself to the situation. There are positive things you can do to exert some control over your work life. I just provided you with five positive actions you can take to help ease the tension in this situation and to stay mentally and physically healthy.

On a final note, all of us possess the ability to go off the rails. If you think you're immune, you're deluding yourself. No one's perfect, so we shouldn't demand it of ourselves, but we can all strive to be better. Whether we seek to improve ourselves at work or home, sometimes just making the effort is what it takes to get over that hump. By doing so you may just turn that *gutting it out* situation into something manageable, if not downright enjoyable.

▬

Interested in more career dissatisfaction and goal setting information?
Check out the Chapter 4 resources at: https://grumpusmaximus.com/golden-albatross-book-chapter-resources/chapter-4/

Chapter 5

The Opposite
of Gutting It Out

I don't want anyone to think that *gutting it out* is the only path I advocate. It's not, nor could it ever be. As I pointed out in Chapter 3, the entire premise surrounding the *Golden Albatross* inflection point implies a choice that someone makes to stay or leave a pensionable job. Thus, if some people choose to stay and *gut out* a pensionable job, it means others don't or won't. So, if you tried some of the coping mechanisms I recommended in the last chapter and they didn't work, then this chapter is for you.

What the Hell Do You Know, Grumpus?

Now, some of my readers may wonder what a guy like me, who chose to *gut it out*, understands about making the alternative decision to leave. That's a fair point. My reply is that people leave the military all the time without earning their pension.

The last time I checked, roughly 80% of active-duty U.S. military personnel fall into this category. Some of those who leave choose to spend enough time in the Reserves or National Guard to earn a different type of pension, but many more do not. Indeed, I've even helped a few people transition directly from active duty to civilian life because it was the right decision for them. More to the point, I've observed numerous other people leave the military without earning a pension. As a result, I believe that I've developed both an appreciation for the right and the wrong reasons for leaving a pensionable job, as well as some good tips for those who do.

The Good

Let's talk about good reasons for leaving a pensionable job first. I'll list my top five, but please understand that, depending on your situation, there might be many other factors at play:

1. **Your Job Has Proven to Be Bad for Your Health.** Take it from someone who has suffered documented mental and physical damage from his chosen profession—at some point, enough is enough. That isn't to say people shouldn't try to reconcile health issues through negotiation with their employers, like requesting a change of responsibilities within an organization. On the other hand, it is to say that at some point every person needs to judge for themselves how much of their precious health the compensation associated with their job is worth. That is very much a *worth vs. worth it* decision, as I described in Chapter 2. Maybe that's made easier by a doctor's diagnosis, or it's something more subjective. Either way, as far as I can tell, you only get one life and one body with which to live it. Until we get to re-sleeve into new bodies like in *Altered Carbon*, that is.

2. **Family.** What's the old saying? *You can choose your friends, but you can't choose your family.* It turns out that may not be the case when it comes to professional versus family issues. You may have a choice, and if you do, you might choose family. For instance, you may want to grow your family. Therefore, leaving a profession to bear and raise children may make the most sense. I've seen this issue play out positively with Mrs. Grumpus. She ultimately left her

profession because we wanted to have kids. Although it was rocky at first, it truly proved the best decision.

    a. On a more negative note, bad shit happens. Family members get sick or die. Parents get old and infirm. Children prove too hard to raise while working. Whatever the case may be, a person may not feel like they have a choice. All I can say is that in my experience it's a rare day when choosing family doesn't prove to be the best decision.

    b. Don't get me wrong, I'm not saying that a young person should sacrifice their hopes and dreams merely because mommy or daddy doesn't want them to fly too far from the nest. What I'm saying is that if you've been out there and proven yourself already, and family issues intervene, don't regret choosing family. You'll almost always have more time to work. You will never get a second chance to hold a parent's hand as they pass away, or help your child navigate those awkward teenage years.

3. **Better Opportunities.** If you're actively researching career and retirement advice, you're in an exceptional minority of the working population, at least in the United States. Don't let it go to your head, because it's a low bar.

    a. That said, it probably means that you have other exceptional talents and abilities. Those talents and abilities might prove so useful to other organizations that they may want to compensate you more than your current employer. Or, alternatively, you may have nurtured those exceptional traits to the point where it's time to employ them yourself. Whatever the case may be, don't be afraid to seize the opportunity if it presents itself, or if you manufacture the opportunity yourself.

b. I listen to a lot of podcasts. A number of them recently marked the 10th anniversary of the Financial Crisis and Great Recession. One of them, in particular, pointed out the following disturbing fact. Despite the subsequent historically long bull market, and near historic unemployment, the majority of U.S. workers who lived through the 2008 and 2009 Financial Crisis and Great Recession are still afraid to switch jobs! Don't let that be you, because like Dr. Seuss might say, *a better tomorrow is on its way.*

c. One word of caution, make sure you calculate the Present Value (PV) or Future Value (FV) of your pension before leaving that job for one that pays more annually without that benefit. Depending on the conditions of the pension, it may turn out that the lower-paying job's compensation is worth more in the long run than the higher paying job without decades of pension cash on the back end. Don't worry if you don't know how to make those calculations. I will show you how in several upcoming chapters.

4. **Your Pension Is Not Safe.** It should go without saying that if your pension system is in financial trouble, then you should (at least partially) discount its value from your *worth vs. worth it* decision-making process. I'll leave the decision of how much you should discount it up to you. Again, don't worry if you don't know how to research the safety of your pension fund. I will show you how to do it two chapters from now. If you can't wait that long then skip to Chapter 7. From there, if you don't know how to factor that lack of safety into a mathematical valuation of your pension, you should check out Chapter 12. Just bear in mind that by skipping ahead you run the risk of missing out on a lot of context.

5. **You Are Already Financially Independent (FI).** Disciplined saving, common sense investing, and compounding growth deliver numerous advantages to people who can harness those powers. Among them is the flexibility to quit a pensionable career (before full vestment) if they've already accumulated enough wealth to live on for the remainder of their years. That isn't to say they'll never work again. However, they can certainly afford to work for less compensation and more fulfillment.

   a. If you don't know how to determine if you've hit FI, I got you covered. Refer back to the *Gap Number* references I made in Chapter 3, along with the references I listed in the end of Chapter 3 resources link. Alternatively, you can just keep reading since I cover the concept of the *Gap Number* in upcoming chapters.

   b. If you are FI, but you find that you're still working a pensionable job, you should probably ask yourself "Why?" Any answer other than, "I love this shit," or "It's my life's calling," or "It fulfills me and I'd do it for free," may make examining some alternatives a worthwhile exercise.

The Bad

OK, since I discussed several good reasons, let's talk about some bad reasons for leaving a pensionable career.

1. **You Hate Your Job.** In my less-than-humble opinion, hating your job in and of itself is not a valid reason to leave a pensionable career. A decision to leave a job should, in part, be based on facts and valuations rather than feelings. Feelings, especially negative ones, are hard to value. And as I stated before, the decision to stay or go is a value decision.

a. My psychologist recently told me that feelings like anger and hate are secondary emotions. They are triggered by a base emotion like shame or guilt. As a result, I'd recommend stripping your issue down to the root cause(s). What specifically do you hate about the job? Is it a boss? Co-workers? Workload? Stress? Company culture? What other emotions are triggered inside you by these people, places, or things? Once you identify the root causes of your feelings, then you need to determine if they can be addressed. Furthermore, you need to attempt to address them. At the end of the day, you may not be able to reconcile the issues, but at least you will have tried. After determining whether the issues are reconcilable, then you can make the value decision of whether you should stay or go.

b. As an aside, which answer to the question of *"Why did you leave your last job?"* sounds better in a follow-on job interview:

   i. I left my job because I hated it.

   ii. I left my job because I couldn't reconcile the differences between my values and the values of the XXXX Corporation. Once I started to work there, I discovered that (insert your negative reason here). Despite repeated attempts to engage management about the corporate culture, I was unable to make any headway. I finally realized that no amount of money in the world was worth my (insert positive reference like "integrity" here). As a result, I decided to leave.

2. **You Got in An Argument.** I know that almost everyone dreams at some point of singing *"Take This Job and Shove It,"* flipping their boss the bird (or the Vs), and quitting. However, I would counsel more

level-headed behavior than that. I'd even counsel better behavior than what JL Collins describes in his book *The Simple Path to Wealth* when he discusses the power of *F.U. Money*. He quit after getting in an argument with his boss, knowing he had enough money saved to allow him and his family to live for years without the need for employment.

    a.   I could list any number of reasons why a person should quit on better terms than in the heat of an argument—from professionalism to the self-serving need to obtain references from your current employer for your next job—but you can research those reasons if you're truly interested. Instead, I'll simply circle back to my previous point: If a person quits on an impulse, they probably didn't make a value decision on whether or not the job (and pension) was worth it.

3. **Or Worse...Someone Called Your Bluff.** Be careful when making ultimatums. I get that integrity is important. I score way high on the ethical scale whenever I take those sorts of tests. It's one thing if there's some fundamentally shady shit going on at your work, and you confront your boss with "do something or else I'll quit and let everyone know why on the way out." However, every disagreement within a workplace doesn't need to end in "or else." If you speak your piece, are listened to, but management chooses a different direction, then it's probably time to shut up and row. Or, if you prefer a military metaphor, you should "choose your hill carefully."

4. **You Refuse to Apologize.** Ask Mrs. Grumpus and she'll tell you; I hate to apologize. I'm a typical meat-eating male military officer. To me, apologizing is a sign of weakness. At least, that's how I used to view it. My new and improved, post-mental breakdown, touchy-feely side realizes how big a mistake that was. I'm trying hard to change by listening more, talking less, and apologizing when I'm

wrong. Doing so has significantly improved my interactions with family and co-workers...well, at least my co-workers. I'm still working on the family part. However, the whole point of that long segue is: don't let an inability to apologize be your reason for quitting a pensionable job. That pension is too valuable, and stubbornness is not.

Other Considerations

Hopefully, you get the point that not all reasons for quitting a pensionable job are good. Nor are they of good value. In any case, let's move on and assume you've got good reasons for not *gutting out* a pensionable career. What should you do next?

I'm glad you asked because in this case, I have a lot of personal experience from interviewing numerous military members before they leave the service. I share just a few of my best nuggets below, many of which will seem like familiar themes from the previous chapter.

1. **Make a Plan.** I've published entire articles about the power of a written plan. I also explained the science behind it in Chapter 4. That said, any U.S. military officer or senior enlisted leader who has ever conducted an exit interview with a more junior Soldier, Sailor, Airman, or Marine can attest to the following fact. The first question we are taught to ask outgoing personnel is "what's your plan?" It's not rhetorical. All personnel who intend to leave or retire must go through a course on how to successfully separate from the service. To successfully pass the course attendees must write down their post-military transition plan. Furthermore, it must be reviewed by the military's version of a guidance counselor. Thus, the military requires exiting service members to transform their *ideas* for post-service life into a *written plan*. I can only presume that

the Department of Defense (DoD) requires this because it knows how powerful writing something down can be.

2. **Make a Backup Plan.** There's an old military adage that no plan survives first contact with the enemy. As a result, you should plan for the failure of, or at least serious modification to, your original plan. The military has numerous names for this type of back up planning including branch planning (like the branches on a tree limb) and prudent planning. Whatever you choose to call it, don't expect failure but know what to do when it heads your way due to circumstances beyond your control. For instance, are you leaving your current job for new employment at the tail end of the economy's current business cycle? If so, do you know what your new organization's layoff policy will be during the next recession? Do they lay off the newest hires first? If they don't have a policy, what does historical precedent tell you? The bottom line here is that you shouldn't stake all your fortunes on one opportunity.

3. **Don't Wait to Execute Parts of Your Plan.** This one gets a little tricky for government workers since often there are ethical guidelines for the type of post-public service employment we can take upon exit. That said, within reason, and in line with federal, state, or local law, do what you can to execute your plan now. Certainly, if you're leaving for other employment, make sure that it's secure. If you're leaving to start your own business, start it as a side hustle and make sure it's sustainable. Ask yourself, "Can I live on this level of income for the next 3, 6, and 12 months?" and "Do I even like this side hustle now that I'm doing it for the money?" Whatever the case may be, don't wait until your current paycheck stops before putting that plan into action...unless the law forces you to.

4. **Take Full Advantage of Current Training Opportunities.** Many employers offer employees opportunities to better themselves, or their skill sets, while on the organization's time. This is something you as an employee should be doing regardless of your intent to stay at your current organization. However, if you know you're going to leave, why not take advantage of those opportunities before your exit? I'm not advocating that you use your department's entire travel budget to attend the training that you need for your new employer. That wouldn't be ethical. However, if your employer allows it, and there's an opportunity to do so, why not get your Lean Six Sigma® certification? Or bone up on those spreadsheet skills? In this day and age, especially in the private sector, there's an expectation that a company will experience a certain amount of attrition among its workforce. Despite that, they still offer in-house training opportunities to anyone who wants to attend. You should take advantage of this benefit.

5. **Depart on Good Terms.** This will seem ironic coming from someone who just advocated for people to take advantage of training opportunities before exiting their current job, but make sure you depart on good terms from your current employer. If I had to rank the previous point I made with the current point I'm making, I consider an amicable departure from your current employer far more important than taking advantage of training opportunities.

   a. I can't tell you the number of times I've written an endorsement for a previous military member who served with me, or under my leadership. Honestly. My memory is like Swiss cheese these days. That said, I could tell you (but won't) the exact number of times I've either politely declined, or intentionally ignored, those requests. Thus, it should come as no surprise that how those people ended their service had a lot to do with the decision I made. Bosses are people after all. People tend to remember their last interaction with a co-worker, and not their co-worker's entire work history. Whether or not that's fair is immaterial for this discussion.

BEST. PLAN. EVER.

Before ending this chapter, let me tell you the best plan for leaving military service that I have ever heard. After I returned from Afghanistan in 2013, but prior to transferring to Europe, I was sitting in the personal property office of my local base. I was trying to arrange the move of my family's household goods. I happened to sit down next to a young E-5 who was probably ending his initial four-year commitment. We struck up a conversation and I asked him what he was waiting for. He told me he was arranging his final move because he was leaving the service so, like all good leaders, I asked him about his post-service plan.

Now, I fully expected him to tell me he was going [back] to school. In my experience, that's the usual answer I get from someone at his age and rank who's decided to leave the service. That's not the answer I got at all. It was yet another example in my life of how misleading it can be to judge a book by its cover.

This particular E-5's answer was that he and his wife were moving back to the area in which they grew up. That's not the surprising part. The surprising part was that he had already accepted an offer of employment at a local gas turbine power plant. Those were the skills he'd acquired while in the service. Much to his credit, he'd directly translated those to immediate employment in the civilian world. He further revealed that his starting salary would easily double his current salary in the military—not to mention the rapid opportunities to make much more.

This E-5 was understandably excited, and to tell you the truth, I was excited for him. I told him that was by far the best plan I had ever heard of, and meant it. I only wish I had offered to keep in touch, just to see how his life turned out. However, I like to think he's making bank, loving his job, providing for his family, and all without the requirement of a college education. BEST. PLAN. EVER.

Interested in more military or civilian career transition information?
Check out the Chapter 5 resources at: https://grumpusmaximus.com/golden-albatross-book-chapter-resources/chapter-5/

Chapter 6

Mental Health, Sad Work, and Stuff

A Promise Fulfilled

Before moving onto Part 2 of this book, I want to weave together several of the themes I addressed in Part 1 with another story. It's a story I promised to tell in greater detail back in Chapters 1 and 3.

In Chapter 5 I stated that it's legitimate to leave a pensionable job if it proves harmful to your health. I also stated that you should trust me since I have documented mental and physical damage from my chosen (pensionable) profession. What I left unsaid in Chapter 5, but stated in the Introduction and Chapter 3, is that I didn't leave my job despite that damage.

In hindsight, and as you're about to find out, I probably should have left the military. Or, more charitably put, I should have at least included the option to leave active duty in my decision-making process. I didn't though, and I have to live with those consequences.

However, *you* can learn from my mistakes. You're hopefully early enough into your *Golden Albatross* moment that you can take the hard lessons I learned and apply them to achieve different (happier) outcomes. Not only that, but you're now equipped with the tools I discussed in the last several chapters. These are tools I neglected to equip myself with before my *Golden Albatross* moment—which may (in part) explain the outcome.

Fair warning, this isn't a feel-good story. Rather, it's a cautionary tale. So, if you need to recharge your coffee cup or your emotional energy banks, now's a good time to do it.

I Am Grumpus Max-ba-bomb . . .

. . . and I am here to make you think about work and get sad and stuff.

In early December 2012, I was scheduled to deploy to Afghanistan but missed my intended deployment date by a week. The night before my original deployment date Mrs. Grumpus and I left our first child with a babysitter and attended an end of 1st-trimester check-up with Mrs. Grumpus's midwife. We had planned the routine appointment as a final special moment before my deployment. It proved final and special, but for all the wrong reasons. That evening we discovered Mrs. Grumpus had miscarried.

The event emotionally devastated both of us. The relatively problem-free first pregnancy that produced our 10+ pound first child lulled us into a false sense of security for the second. As a result, we weren't prepared for the emotional ton of bricks dropped on us that night. The thought of my babbling, tear-filled phone call to our babysitter after we discovered the results still makes me tear-up today.

Immediate Actions

I had experienced some bad moments in my life before that night. I was almost killed at 13 years old in an accident that left my body mangled. A friend, co-worker, and mentor of mine was killed in Iraq in 2003. And, as I related in Chapter 2, I nearly killed myself while on a mission in 2009. However, nothing in my life, before or since, compares to the collective sadness my wife and I shared that evening or in the following days.

The miscarriage required several small medical procedures, not all of which were completed before I deployed. The week's delay to my deployment provided just enough time to ensure Mrs. Grumpus got through the primary medical procedure and linked up with her mental health professional. She had suffered through serious postpartum depression after our first child, so I considered this vital. And then I deployed as an Individual Augmentee (IA) for four months to a war most Americans had forgotten about, and whose course of events I was unable to affect in the least.

As bitter as I feel about that deployment, the truth is I was provided an opportunity to skip it. The consequences to my career would have been severe, but I could have done it. I didn't skip the deployment though. Even though it wasn't my unit in Afghanistan, the person I was meant to replace at that unit was from my organization and had a pregnant wife at home. Thus, I felt an obligation to meet the commitment I'd made. More to the point though, and as awful as it sounds, I needed the deployment.

Where Was My Mind?

Backtracking a bit, following the deployment in 2009 (that I discussed in Chapter 2) I was burned out. I had spent 13 months deployed between 2007 and 2009, and another 5 months training away from home. Thus, I took advantage of a change of duty station and unit in late 2009 to sit the war(s) out for a few years.

Initially, the time off was put to good use. My wife and I spent a lot of 2010 repairing some of the inevitable damage that my previous deployments caused our marriage. Mrs. Grumpus and I got right with each other through counseling, then decided to try for our first child. That happened quickly and we had our first by the spring of 2011. Parenting (after postpartum depression) proved to be so fulfilling that we decided to try for another.

While all that was going on, I continued to work hard at my new unit but never stuck my hand in the air for a deployment. Everyone was deploying in one capacity or another. It was just a matter of time before my number came up, so I enjoyed the time at home until my turn came. In the meantime, as a result of hard work (and a bit of luck), I finagled a follow-on tour to a choice job in Europe that would start in mid-2013.

At that point, it was mid-2012, and I realized that I needed to deploy to stay competitive for my next promotion. My follow-on job in Europe wasn't going to help my chances of promotion. Plus, while I'd sat on the sidelines for three years, my peers continued to deploy. Although Iraq had shut down by that point (before ramping up again for ISIS) the surge to Afghanistan had my organization deploying hot and heavy. If I didn't deploy before heading to Europe, the chances of staying competitive for promotion looked slim. Conversely, if I did deploy, I believed I'd be promoted without a problem.

Don't get me wrong. I didn't want the promotion so I could keep climbing the ranks. My concerns were far more practical. The way I saw it at the time, not promoting would have caused a whole slew of problems with my ability to provide for my expanding family. This included the potential of missing out on the all-important 20-year mark required for a military pension and a lifetime of subsidized healthcare.

Thus, by the time I pulled my head away from my family in the summer of 2012, I was inside 12 months from departing my current command for Europe while looking for a deployment with a pregnant wife. At the time I felt fortunate to find a deployment that worked out perfectly—a short four months to Afghanistan. I'd be back for the birth and in time to move the family to Europe. What could go wrong? Well, as we found out in Chapter 2, whenever I ask that rhetorical question, just about everything.

A Few Last Stops on the Way Down

I didn't know it at the time, but the circumstances under which I deployed after the miscarriage destroyed any remaining mental resilience left in my arsenal. PTS was not only likely but the natural conclusion to these events. Like a dam with one too many fissures, or the incoming tide washing away a sandcastle, the results proved slow but inevitable. I have no idea how, but I struggled on for three more years before my mental breakdown in the spring of 2016, after which, I begrudgingly reached out for help. Yet, I'm getting ahead of myself.

By the time I returned from Afghanistan in the spring of 2013, my wife had moved on emotionally, and the family had a trans-Atlantic change of duty station to execute. So, I did what any military-age male with my demeanor does...shoved those shitty feelings surrounding the miscarriage deep down into my emotional rucksack and Charlie Miked (Continued Mission). When the dam finally burst, I was three years on, almost ready to change duty stations again.

Hindsight is 20/20

Despite carrying myself with the outward appearance of calm for the majority of those three years in Europe, inside I was an emotional wreck. Leakage in the form of erratic and uncontrollable angry outbursts, or random tear-filled moments, appeared more frequently.

My family took the brunt of it, but not all of it. I scared, to within an inch of his life, some "asshole" who dared block my driveway with his car one day (when Mrs. Grumpus was pregnant with our second child). I also fought with my older brother at a family reunion for daring to curse in front of our first child. Those are just two of the more egregious examples of my behavior. Of course, I realize now that over-protectiveness of your family is textbook PTS behavior for military personnel.

My physical health started to deteriorate as well. Sudden onset acid reflux was first. I had never experienced acid reflux in my life but started throwing up routinely. After numerous tests (which verified it was real, not psychosomatic), and months of medication, I finally resorted to surgery. I also suffered from a barrage of sinus infections for 2+ years, which again required surgery.

Only after my mental breakdown did I finally seek professional psychiatric help. The breakdown wasn't as dramatic as Ed Norton's character in *Fight Club* when he realized he was Tyler Durden, but it was emotional and hard. What can I say? Talking about feelings and sad stuff ain't easy for a guy like me. However, for the good of myself and my family, I did it, learning a thing or two along the way.

Therapy, THER-a-PEE

Therapy helped, but it wasn't the cure-all I wanted it to be. What it did do was help me understand some of the core problems. For example, I never properly mourned the miscarriage. This led to immense sadness and guilt...sadness over losing a child I already loved, and guilt about deploying and "abandoning" my wife due to the perceived demands of my career.

Like the grooves on a vinyl album, the sadness had worn an indelible impression on my psyche and soul. I doubt those will ever fade. When something triggers my sadness, it feels as if a hole opens up in my chest. That hole seems as deep as the one created the night Mrs. Grumpus and I learned of the miscarriage. It's inexplicable and doesn't appear to be going away anytime soon. All I know is some things tend to set it off, like songs, movies, television, discussions, or books which address the death of a child. I tend to avoid those things these days.

"Wars Make Not One Great"

The guilt is something different altogether. As my therapist pointed out, there were completely rational reasons as to why I had to follow through with the commitment I made to deploy to Afghanistan. Not only would there have been repercussions for not deploying, but by deploying I was ensuring long-term financial security for my family by staying competitive for promotion.

My therapist pushed me to have the same conversation with Mrs. Grumpus, so I could hear firsthand if she understood the situation in the same terms. Much to Mrs. Grumpus's credit, when I eventually talked with her, she told me the same thing my therapist did—that she understood the reasons why I deployed, and supported them.

However, none of that, the discussions with the therapist or Mrs. Grumpus, did much to wash away how much I felt like...a goddamned mercenary. In case you were wondering, the Merriam-Webster online dictionary defines a mercenary as "one that serves merely for wages." The International Committee of the Red Cross notes that a mercenary, "is motivated to take part in the hostilities essentially by the desire for private gain."

Just to be clear, that's not why I originally joined the U.S. military. I joined to serve, give back to my country, and be a part of something greater than myself. However, when all was said and done, my deployment to Afghanistan boiled down to a need for money or other forms of payment.

Extrapolating those feelings up a level, 13 years into my military service, my career had come down to nothing more than a mercenary endeavor to secure my family's financial future. The irony that Afghanistan proved the burial place of the noble pretenses surrounding my service isn't lost on me. There's no doubt many a Macedonian and British soldier felt the same during their campaigns in those lands.

The Butcher's Bill

Some jobs demand more than others on a routine basis. At some point, all jobs make demands that may prove too much for a person to take. I should have said "enough" in December 2012, but I had no alternative paradigm. This deployment was before my discovery of FI and JL Collins' concept of *F.U. money*. Thus, I couldn't see my way past the situation.

As I mentioned in Chapter 3, if I hadn't squandered a significant chunk of money on a condominium in Southern California at the height of the housing market in 2004, things might have turned out differently. That money may have given me the confidence to say "no mas," even without an understanding of the Principles of FI or something like the book *The Simple Path to Wealth* as a guide.

Things didn't play out that way though. There was no significant chunk of money, and certainly no understanding on my part of the alternatives. Plus, my life and identity were invested in the idea of serving in the military. In other words, I had built a lot of momentum in the trajectory I was on.

Instead, I chose to stuff more and more into my emotional rucksack. Like some sin-eater gorging itself on the transgressions of others with no understanding of the burden, I thought I could shove everything down and soldier on. I believed I had to carry my family on my shoulders and be their sole provider. I couldn't, and this added to my pain, regardless of how unrealistic or unachievable that belief proved to be.

In hindsight, the scariest realization from all of this was the fact that I never truly considered *not* going to Afghanistan. Whether I had go fever or my tendency as a linear problem solver had taken over at that point, I was deploying. As an example of just how bad this mentality was, my mother, viewing this storm from many states away, talked me into simply requesting a week's delay in my deployment. Fast forward three years, it's no wonder I started to leak errant behavior, and then finally broke down. The only wonder is how I didn't break down earlier.

Unlike Yoda's sage wisdom, it wasn't fear that led me to the Dark Side, but guilt. In case you don't remember, or never saw, *Star Wars*, I've drawn you a diagram:

GUILT —> ANGER —> HATE —> DARK SIDE

My guilt over deploying after the miscarriage led to anger. Not that I ever needed more fuel for my anger, but now I was angry about *everything* and didn't know why. In hindsight, it's easy to see that I was the problem. That anger transitioned into hate, hate of self and everyone around me. That hate led to the Dark Side and ultimately my breakdown.

Don't Try This at Home, Kids

I found myself deploying in December 2012, a week after my wife miscarried because I erroneously believed I had no alternative when it came to securing my family's financial future. That decision caused serious damage to my psyche and self-esteem. It's too late for me, but it may not be too late for you. While I pick up the pieces, you can avoid crashing in the first place by refusing to place a job above your mental health, your physical health, or your family's happiness. The good news is that if you're reading this, you've already done more to explore a different way than I ever did before deploying to Afghanistan.

In reality, I had plenty of choices. While I certainly wasn't living my financial life intentionally at that point, it's not like we were destitute or I was unemployable. As described in Chapter 3, Mrs. Grumpus and I had tracked and saved our money for years. We lived well below our means, even with a child. We had alternatives such as running the risk of not promoting by not deploying, transitioning to the reserves, or leaving the service for the civilian world.

But, I couldn't grasp the alternatives conceptually because I hadn't taken the time to educate myself. I wasn't listening to personal finance podcasts, reading financial books or blogs. While I lacked the financial knowledge, I also lacked the self-belief. I had no blog through which I could exercise other interests or my writing abilities. My life revolved around going from home to work and work to home, with some surfing in between. Other than the counseling I did with Mrs. Grumpus to get ready for our first child, I wasn't doing much to make myself a more well-rounded person.

Epilogue

I originally posted the majority of what you just read on my blog in the immediate aftermath of my first (and to date biggest) podcast interview. The interview was with Brad Barrett and Jonathan Mendonsa of the ChooseFI Podcast. On the podcast, I talked about some of my mental health struggles, how they related to my pensionable career, and the interplay with my *Golden Albatross* decision. However,

I didn't get into the explicit traumatic events that caused my PTS.

As often happens after bloggers are interviewed on popular podcasts, I knew I was in for a temporary, but big, increase in readership. Thus, I knew I had a platform for one or two weeks to publish something that would reach far beyond my normal readership. Therefore, I chose to follow up on my references in the podcast about my mental health struggles with a post about the specific events that caused my PTS, forced the onset of my mental breakdown, and heralded my *Golden Albatross* moment.

Why? For one, I hadn't talked about the causes of my PTS specifically on my blog by that point. I had alluded to them, but had never come out and explicitly stated that I had PTS because of X, Y, and Z. So, I felt like I owed it to my readers.

That said, I also felt like I owed it to anyone in the ChooseFI audience who might be suffering in silence with mental health issues— especially those suffering from PTS. I had no way of confirming, but I suspected that the ChooseFI audience included more than a few police, firefighters, and military personnel. These are the types of pensionable workers, with higher than normal rates of mental health issues, I often picture as my audience when writing my posts. It seemed like a great opportunity to reach them.

Despite wanting to help, it was the most difficult post I've ever written. Even though I blog under a pseudonym, from the moment I hit the publish button it felt like a massive public airing of some intensely personal issues. As a result, I was apprehensive about the response.

I shouldn't have worried though. The response was not only motivating but also 100% positive. In fact, between the podcast and that article, I achieved far more than I ever hoped. Numerous readers reached out to me about their mental health and/or financial issues, some of whom turned into true friends. In many ways, it's a gift that keeps on giving, and now I'm passing it on to you.

I had grown complacent, and stupidly ignored the warning that life provided me in 2009. My brush with death while on that 2009 mission seriously shook my belief in the "cause," but I never gave those doubts serious consideration for the alternatives they might hold. Maybe I was afraid, or just emotionally dumb. Either way, my lack of proactivity and my uninformed beliefs contributed heavily to the circumstances and the decision I made back in December 2012. It's a place I never wish to find myself again, and a place I hope you never find yourself.

Herein Ends Part 1 of the Book

You picked up, downloaded, or decided to listen to this book for a reason. What was that reason? Was it something positive or negative? Given my subtitle, I would hazard a guess and say it's something negative. I certainly hope that's not the case, but with a Nom de Guerre like Grumpus Maximus, is it any surprise that I'd concentrate on the negative?

What exactly drives your negative feelings about your pensionable job? Can those root causes be addressed or reconciled? Have you tried? If irreconcilable, where do the negative feelings range on the scale of importance? What's most important to you? What have you done to mitigate those feelings?

At the end of the day, I can only help so much. I can't answer the above questions, only you can. Granted, I recommended some coping strategies that might help you better determine what's going on. Maybe with those strategies, you can maneuver through this period of your career while still sticking with the pensionable job. Maybe not. That's your decision to make, not mine. Yet...before you make that decision, there's more to consider. There's another side of the *worth vs. worth it* equation we need to address. So, don't do anything rash. Just let those feelings percolate while you read or listen onwards, or downwards, as the case may be.

Interested in more work-related mental health information or hearing Grumpus Maximus talk about mental health and work? Check out the Chapter 6 resources at: https://grumpusmaximus.com/golden-albatross-book-chapter-resources/chapter-6/

THE GOLDEN ALBATROSS

PART TWO

Chapter 7

Is Your Pension Safe?

Welcome to Part 2 of the Book!

Part 1 introduced you to the concept of the *Golden Albatross* inflection point. It's a conundrum that I believe many people in pensionable career fields hit at some point in their work life. That inflection point manifests itself as a *worth vs. worth it* decision. I've turned that decision into an equation. Part of the equation is subjective; the other part is objective.

Following my explanation of the *Golden Albatross*, I moved on to some practical methods for categorizing and (potentially) mitigating the negative impacts and emotions surrounding your job. I also introduced you to my list of valid reasons for quitting a pensionable career. I ended Part 1 with more questions than a police detective interrogating a murder suspect—questions meant to help you quantify and qualify the negative impacts and emotions you might be experiencing in your pensionable job.

That said, it's time to turn our attention to the more objective side of the equation, which centers on determining your pension's worth. Another word for worth is *value*, which is the term I use a lot in the following chapters. However, before moving into the chapters where I demonstrate how to determine a pension's value (or worth), I want to discuss the issue of pension safety.

Why Start with Pension Safety?

If someone determines that their pension is not safe, it may influence their decision to leave their job so heavily that further research into the value of their pension might not be needed. Of course, life isn't typically that black or white. There can be a lot of grey when it comes to determining just how safe a pension is. I've learned quite a bit on the topic over the years. That's mostly because the pension industry is constantly evolving and adapting.

Regardless, I still think the question of pension safety is the most practical starting place for the objective side of the *worth vs. worth it* equation. If nothing else, it makes for a great entrée into the various aspects of pensions themselves.

Are Pensions at Risk?

At the risk of sounding like Captain Obvious, I think it's important to point out that if you can't rely on your pension to be there in retirement, then you shouldn't rely on it when planning for FI. Yes, I know that's common sense, but you know what I say about common sense? If it was common, we'd just call it sense.

It shouldn't be news to anyone who works in the U.S. that pensions are no longer a common practice in corporate America. The public sector is often referred to as the last bastion of pensions in the United States and has started to phase them out, too. There are multiple reasons for these phase-outs, some of which I touch upon next. Despite that, some of us will earn pensions. *If* you can count on that pension to materialize on time and in the correct amount, it could prove decisive in achieving FI. Unfortunately, that is an increasingly big *if* in today's fiscal environment.

Illustration: Captain Obvious

Management

With that said, not everyone's pension is in peril. So, what makes one pension safer than another? One separating factor is management. Well-run pensions that have more assets than liabilities (i.e. pensions that have a funding rate of 100% or higher) are much safer and more reliable than those that don't. Sound contribution requirements and realistic projected rates of return also serve as good indicators of a well-managed fund. Unfortunately, as we'll soon discuss, there are certain types of pensions where this type of good management is less common than others.

Another factor separating pensions is the bankroll of the plan's sponsor. In other words, how much money does a sponsor have to fund pension shortfalls that the investment portfolio and contributions can't cover? Until recently, government-sponsored public pensions were typically considered those with the deepest pockets. This was due to the government's ability to levy taxes. In a post-Great Recession world, that no longer rings true. Like their corporate counterparts, fewer governments can afford the cost of DBPs.

The 80% Myth

In recent decades a myth has developed about the health of U.S. pension funds based on their funding rate. Specifically, those with 80% of their liabilities funded are considered healthy. That contrasts sharply with my statement above that well-run pension funds are those with more assets than liabilities (i.e. pensions funded at 100% or higher). The problem is the term *liabilities*. In the pension world that term not only includes current retirees drawing from the fund now, but current workers who will retire and draw upon the fund in the future.

Since no one can predict the future with absolute accuracy, it's hard for pension funds to know exactly how much money they should set aside to pay future pensioners. A fund with 100% of future predicted liabilities covered in 2020 might end up with too much money in 2030. Several events might cause this to occur. For instance, if stock market returns prove higher than normal in the intervening decade, a pension fund may find itself awash in cash. A situation like that may also occur if a lot of contributing workers quit right before vesting in their pension.

Now, that's not nearly as likely as the opposite situation (i.e. a 100% funded level in 2020 doesn't translate to enough money to cover all liabilities in 2030), but it could happen. As a result, the pension fund managers in 2030 might look back at the 100% funding level in 2020 and conclude that they could have gotten away with an 80% funded level instead. That's exactly what's going on with the current 80% funding myth across the U.S. Rather than waiting until 2030 to see what the future may bring though, pension funds and some of the government agencies that regulate them, are jumping to the 80% conclusion now.

I'm not making this stuff up! There are actual experts in this field with degrees and other important acronyms at the beginning and/ or end of their names that determine the extent of future liability for pension funds. These experts are called actuaries. Actuaries are mathematicians whose sole job is to determine the answers for future math problems based on current numbers. In other words, they use current data and statistics to determine future monetary risk for industries such as finance, insurance, and pension funds. They've developed an entire science around the techniques they use, known as actuarial science.

Therefore, it's important to note that in July 2012, the American Academy of Actuaries published the following points about pension funding in their Issue Brief entitled "The 80% Pension Funding Standard Myth":

- Frequent unchallenged references to 80% funding as a healthy level threaten to create a mythic standard.

- No single level of funding should be identified as a defining line between a "healthy" and an "unhealthy" pension plan. Funded ratios are a point-in-time measurement.

- The movement or trend of the funded ratio is as important as the absolute level.

- Most plans should have the objective of accumulating assets equal to 100% of a relevant pension obligation.

- The financial health of a pension plan depends on many factors in addition to funded status—particularly the size of any shortfall compared with the resources of the plan sponsor.

For the most part, these findings jive with everything I just said above, with one exception. They note that the trend in funding levels is more important than the actual percentage of funded liabilities when considering the stability of a fund. So, a fund that's chronically underfunded, or with a funding ratio that's getting worse instead of better, would be an indicator of poor health. The opposite would be true for a fund with increasingly better funding levels over time. I don't think that's anything earth-shattering. That's just good mathematically-based analysis.

Public Pension Health: Federal, State, and Local Level

If you're a U.S. Federal employee, the only issue you need to consider when determining the safety of your Federal Employees Retirement System (FERS) pension, or your military pension, is the solvency of the U.S. government. The U.S. government, for better or worse, always pays its debts—if not technically on time, then at least with back interest. Your future pension is one of many U.S. government debts. Thus, about the only time you might remotely worry about your pension is when issues like U.S. debt limit ceilings, balanced budgets, and tax cuts with offsets are being debated in Congress. That said, it's probably worth keeping an eye on inflation. Even though federal pensions come with Cost of Living (COL) increases, rampant inflation can be a killer.

The United States isn't the only country that always meets its financial obligations. According to Investopedia, as of 2011 Canada, Denmark, Belgium, Finland, Malaysia, Mauritius, New Zealand, Norway, Singapore, Switzerland, and England (I assume they mean the UK) had never defaulted on sovereign debt. That isn't to say those countries never faced a financial crisis. Nor am I saying they've never stiffed their federal pensioners. What I'm saying is that their ability to keep their finances in order speaks well to the future likelihood they'll pay their federal pensioners.

Conversely, if you are an employee of the Greek, Spanish, or Italian federal governments and are owed a federal pension, future pension obligations probably take on more importance every time a member of the European Central Bank comes to town. Argentina and Brazil are other countries where discussions about the security of federal pensions turn sour. Argentina has a particularly long history of defaulting on its domestic debt, which includes pensions.

Move down to the state level in the U.S. and again, depending on the state, your pension may be more or less at risk. When I originally wrote about this in September 2017, state workers in Kentucky were tripping over themselves to retire, due to pending changes in their state's retirement plan. If you're a state worker but never looked into the health of your state's pension plan, do your research. I hope all of you work in New York, South Dakota, Washington D.C., Tennessee, or one of the other handful of well-run states. Unfortunately, I doubt that is the case.

The story is much the same at the county, city, and local levels. Some pensions are well run, but many others are not. Do Detroit, Michigan, or Stockton, California, ring any bells? Both U.S. cities declared bankruptcy after the Great Recession. Their inability to meet pension obligations played a big part in both of those bankruptcies. Overobligating benefits while underfunding those obligations is a sure sign your local government pension plan is in trouble. Taxes don't always save those plans either. At some point, local taxpayers push back, especially if they perceive mismanagement.

If That's The Bad News, What's the Good News?

So, if you stand to earn a public DBP in the U.S., are you doomed? Absolutely not. However, you should start researching your plan's fiscal health now, especially if you are relying on that pension to fund major portions of your retirement and/or to reach FI. Boston College runs an organization called the Center for Retirement Research, and it's a fabulous resource. The site includes links to the Public Plans Database (PPD).

The PPD accounts for over 90% of public sector pension plans. You can search state-by-state, plan-by-plan, and read up on national trends. The database provides you a quick overview of your pension's financial status. In some cases, it also links to the financial documents that pensions publish annually. I hope you find good news when you delve into the facts!

Private Pensions

From the 1980s through the present, the total number of American corporate workers covered by DBPs shrank from 60% to approximately 10% of the workforce. DBPs proved too expensive for corporate America. When the Reagan administration loosened some of the rules regarding pension administration in the 1980s, corporate America saw its opportunity and headed for the exit. It did this through several different mechanisms, including freezing pension funds from new employees and transferring the remaining obligations through mechanisms like Pension Risk Transfer (PRT) to insurance companies. That trend continues. 2017 was a banner year for the number of corporations unloading their pension obligations to insurance companies. If you want to know more about PRT because you think your pension may be subject to that action, take a look at the call-out box on page 78 and the resources at the end of this chapter.

Today's remaining corporate pension plans face the same two hurdles that public pensions face—increased obligations and under-funding. In August 2017, *The Wall Street Journal* reported that the funding gap for all remaining S&P 500 pension plans *"could exceed the previous record set in 2012 when the funding shortfall hit $451 billion."* That headline was based on an S&P 500 Indices report that I've linked at the end of this chapter along with some other resources.

The S&P 500's report is mandatory reading if you work for an S&P 500 company, and a pension is coming your way. Among other things, it contains an appendix of the S&P 500 companies with pension obligations and their status. One interesting note from the report is that, despite today's historically low-interest-rate environment, the shortfalls remain manageable for the near term. Shortfalls will only shrink when interest rates climb.

The report also points out that pension obligations will eventually crest as the remaining Baby Boomers retire and die. Alternatively stated, since most Gen-Xers and Millennials don't have a pension coming their way, corporate pension obligations will slowly shrink as a total percentage of a company's bottom line as Baby Boomer pensioners die off. This will increase corporate fiscal health. So, if you're a Gen-Xer or Millennial, and corporate America owes you a pension, then congratulations! If the pension fund can survive the wave of Baby Boomers retiring, you'll likely get yours.

Pension Risk Transfer (PRT)

Occurs when pension funds transfer some, or all, of their future pension liabilities to an individual or an insurance company. PRT to an individual takes the form of a lump sum payment in which a vested member of the fund accepts a singular Current Value (CV) payment instead of a reoccurring future annuity. When complete, the risk of running out of money in retirement transfers from the pension fund to the individual who took the lump sum.

PRTs to insurance companies are a wholesale transfer of a frozen portion of a pension fund's assets which are obligated against specific future liabilities. By accepting the assets an insurance company accepts the future responsibility to pay affected participants in the frozen plan through either lump sums or annuities. Insurance companies are uniquely positioned to take on pension risk, as it's the same type of risk they manage by providing insurance annuities to individuals. PRTs to insurance companies are typically seamless and risk-neutral for affected pension plan participants unless they choose a lump sum.

The Pension Benefit Guaranty Corporation (PBGC)

One final note about corporate pensions is that the Pension Benefit Guaranty Corporation (PBGC) covers most of them in the U.S. If you think that sounds like an insurance organization, you'd be correct. The U.S. government runs PBGC as an insurance plan for Single-Employer Plans (SEPs) and Multi-Employer Plans (MEPs) in case they fail. Congress commissioned the PBGC in the 1970s to prevent companies (and their pension plans) from leaving workers high and dry when they declared bankruptcy.

What's the difference between a SEP and a MEP? SEPs are funded by only one company like Xerox or FedEx. MEPs are funded by multiple companies like auto manufacturers who employ union members. Thus, an overly simplistic way of thinking about the difference between SEP and MEP is a corporate job versus a union job.

It's extremely important to note that the PBGC has a separate insurance fund for each type of plan (SEP vs. MEP). More importantly, there's a qualitative difference between the funds that every contributor to a private pension needs to understand. While both schemes were underfunded as recently as 2018, the SEP fund was projected to be in the black by no later than 2022. Conversely, the MEP fund was projected to be insolvent by 2025. Thus, if the MEP fund steps in to take over a failing pension fund, pensioners receive drastically reduced monthly payouts.

The bottom line on the PBGC is this: While it's great that the PBGC exists, depending on the type of plan you contribute to, you might be OK or you might be screwed if it's forced to take over your pension fund. If this applies to your situation, I have compiled a list of resources on the PBGC linked at the end of this chapter so you can continue your research.

Bottom Line: How Safe is Your Pension?

Spoiler alert, there's no way I can answer the above question for you. At best, I can point you in the direction where that answer might lie. I believe that's what I've done here. At worst, I've painted such a dismal picture that you're ready to withdraw all your money, head to your closest casino, and "always bet on black." Don't do that.

More to the point, the pension story is not all doom and gloom. Depending on your pension plan, you may be fine. If you look at the data, and you believe that to be the case, check out the resources I listed at the end of the chapter.

On the other hand, if you read this chapter and got a sinking feeling in your stomach, don't despair. First of all, make sure you utilize the resources below and put together the most accurate picture possible of your pension fund's health. This includes obtaining the latest financial report from your pension plan administrator. They must make those available by law.

—

Want to study the pension safety issue further?
Check out the Chapter 7 resources at: https://grumpusmaximus.com/golden-albatross-book-chapter-resources/chapter-7/

Chapter 8

What's Your Pension Worth?

Calculating Your Pension's Worth Ain't Like Dusting Crops

Anybody else exhausted from the last few chapters? I know I am. At 3000 words the last one wasn't concise. Among all those words you may remember my promise to help you determine your pension's worth. Well, the future is now! Or at least partially. I intend to break up the discussion over the next several chapters. Since calculating your pension's worth is more of a *how-to* process, it provides us a welcome pause from staring into the soulless eyes of the *Golden Albatross* and deciding whether or not to shrug it off.

There are three key inputs to determining your pension's worth plus some mathematical formulas. I try to keep it simple because I am not a math genius by any means (liberal arts major here!) and more than likely you are going to use a pension calculator. However, you should understand the inputs and formulas because like Han Solo said in *Star Wars: A New Hope:*

> *Traveling through hyperspace ain't like dusting crops, boy!*
> *Without precise calculations, we could fly right through a star*
> *or bounce too close to a supernova, and that'd end your trip*
> *real quick, wouldn't it?*

Illustration: Calculating your pension's worth ain't like dusting crops.

We don't want your retirement trip ending "real quick," do we? Fortunately, identifying the three inputs is not hard. If you've done any sort of retirement planning, you probably calculated or accounted for these inputs already. Due to their overall importance in your retirement and your potential FI plans, I'd be surprised if you hadn't at least considered them. The three inputs are:

1. The Initial Dollar Value (IDV) of your pension

2. Your pension's interaction with inflation

3. The immediacy of your pension.

Let's tackle each of these inputs in order.

The Initial Dollar Value (IDV)

I think it's important to note (again) that when I refer to a pension throughout this chapter, I mean a Defined Benefit Pension (DBP). Investopedia states:

> In a defined-benefit plan, the employer guarantees that the employee receives a definite amount of benefit upon retirement, regardless of the performance of the underlying investment pool. The employer is liable for a specific flow of pension payments to the retiree (the dollar amount is determined by a formula, usually based on earnings and years of service), and if the assets in the pension plan are not sufficient to pay the benefits, the company is liable for the remainder of the payment.

I'd like you to focus on the portion in the parentheses, and note that there is typically a formula involved. This means you need to find out what your company or organization's retirement formula is before moving any further. That's easy for some of us because the formula is posted online and/or fairly well understood. For others, it might require a trip to Human Resources (HR), or research in your original hiring documentation.

Being in the military, I fall into the former category. I'm under the High Thirty-Six model (aka High Three) which means I earn a pension at twenty years of service worth fifty-percent of the average of my highest three paid years of base pay. Base pay means my taxable pay and doesn't include allowances and special pays. Thus, part of my pension's formula looks like this:

$$[(X + Y + Z) / 3] \times .5 =$$
annual pension dollar amount at 20 years of service

In this case, X, Y, and Z represent my three highest-paid years of base pay.

However, there's an additional consideration. The government adds 2.5% for each year over 20 years of service. Thus, the complete calculation looks like this:

$$[(X + Y + Z) / 3] \times [.5 + (.025 \times Yo)] =$$
annual pension dollar amount at XX years of service

'Yo' represents the number of years over twenty a person served, and XX equals the total number of years served. Thus, if you retire at 30 years, you will earn 75% of the average of your three highest years of base pay.

In preparation for this chapter, I ran an unscientific survey of my Facebook Group (*Golden Albatross* / Golden Handcuffs) members. It turns out the most common method for calculating IDV among this group was the average of their three to five highest paid years multiplied by a specified percentage. Pension plans that linked the percentage by which the salary average is multiplied, to the number of years worked, appeared to be common as well. A few examples from various members in my group included:

- Highest consecutive 5-year compensation average x years of service x 1.35%

- Final average compensation (FAC) x 1.5% (pension factor) x years of service (YOS)

- [(A + B + C) / 3] x .66 = Initial yearly pension with 2% bump in the multiple for each year of service over 25 years; maximum of 100%

Holy cow, I thought I was well compensated, but the last example above comes with an extremely valuable initial multiple, plus an ability to work your way to 100% compensation in 42 years if you want to stay that long.

Sometimes, pensions require a certain number of years at the job to *vest* in the retirement scheme. For instance, the U.S. military pension requires twenty years of service. That all-or-nothing aspect for the pension is sometimes called *cliff vesting*. This means you either serve/ work the required amount of time and get the pension, or you don't.

Not all pensions use *cliff vesting*. Some pensions *partially or gradually vest* a person at a certain number of years on the job, but *fully vest* them many years later. The difference between *partial vesting* and *fully vesting* in a pension may mean a different value calculation is used to determine IDV. Or, it may mean certain types of benefits, like healthcare, are not provided until a person *fully vests*. Either way, it should go without saying that pensions with the fewest number of years required to *fully vest* are better than those that require longer timeframes.

Speaking of healthcare attached to pensions, the above IDV examples do not include Other Post-Retirement Benefits (OPRBs) that may be part of a retirement package. We will discuss how to value those in later chapters. For the moment, we are strictly talking about monetary compensation. Even so, it's easy to see how powerful a role a pension could play in your retirement plans if you can make it to the full vesting point. Often that's a big *IF*. *Full vesting* periods might require 20 years or more of work. Only a few of the pensions from my Facebook group had *full vesting* periods under 25 years.

A lot of people, and especially those seeking Financially Independent Retired Early (FIRE) status, might struggle to work the same job for that long. For them, the decision to stay may come down to a *worth vs. worth it* decision as I addressed in Chapter 2. The IDV, while an important component in determining the answer to the *worth* part of the equation, is not the only factor. Determining the effects of inflation on your pension is just as important.

Inflation's Effect

What is inflation? The Bureau of Labor Statistics (BLS—the U.S. government agency that tracks inflation) states that inflation is "defined as the overall general upward price movement of goods and services in an economy." In layman's terms, it is the word used to describe the trend that typically sees a year-over-year price increase on the stuff you buy. That change may not seem like much in any single year but added up over decades it changes the cost of goods dramatically.

For example, *Star Wars IV: A New Hope* grossed $307,263,857 in domestic U.S. theaters when it originally debuted in 1977. Compare that to the highest domestic grossing film (so far) in the franchise, *Star Wars VII: The Force Awakens*. It grossed $936,662,225 when originally released in 2016.

At face value, this gap seems like a huge difference, but consider how the cost of movie tickets rose over those 39 years. According to an interactive query tool at Davemanual.com, a movie ticket in 1977 cost an average of $2.23. In 2016 that same ticket cost $8.65. Thus, when you adjust the original 1977 gross domestic box office numbers from *A New Hope* ($307,263,857) for inflation, to 2016 dollars, you find *A New Hope* grossed $1,216,922,054. That inflation-adjusted figure far surpases *The Force Awakens*, which means *A New Hope* is the top domestic grossing *Star Wars* franchise movie (so far). Instinctively, this makes sense, given the movie's culturally defining status in the U.S. and around the world.

So, what does inflation do to your pension? Well, if your pension's initial payment amount is not inflation-adjusted, inflation slowly devalues your pension over time. If each year you go to the movies and the tickets keep getting more expensive, but the amount of cash in your pocket remains the same, you'll quickly realize you can't afford to go to the movies anymore. Which sucks, because you'll want to see *Star Wars Episode 20: Great-Grandson of the Last Returned Jedi Who Struck Back* when it's released in 2045.

A few of you well-informed readers might have heard utterances about the death of inflation. It's true that inflation, as measured by the BLS in what is known as the Consumer Price Index for all Urban Workers (CPI-U), has remained below the historical average (3.22%) since the 2008-09 Great Recession. The below chart displays the year-over-year change in CPI-U inflation rates since 2007 by month and annually. The information is from the BLS's website.

YEAR	JAN	FEB	MAR	APR	MAY	JUNE	JULY	AUG	SEPT	OCT	NOV	DEC	ANNUAL
2007	2.1	2.4	2.8	2.6	2.7	2.7	2.4	2.0	2.8	3.5	4.3	4.1	2.8
2008	4.3	4.0	4.0	3.9	4.2	5.0	5.6	5.4	4.9	3.7	1.1	0.1	3.8
2009	0.0	0.2	-0.4	-0.7	-1.3	-1.4	-2.1	-1.5	-1.3	-0.2	1.8	2.7	-0.4
2010	2.6	2.1	2.3	2.2	2.0	1.1	1.2	1.1	1.1	1.2	1.1	1.5	1.6
2011	1.6	2.1	2.7	3.2	3.6	3.6	3.6	3.8	3.9	3.5	3.4	3.0	3.2
2012	2.9	2.9	2.7	2.3	1.7	1.7	1.4	1.7	2.0	2.2	1.8	1.7	2.1
2013	1.6	2.0	1.5	1.1	1.4	1.8	2.0	1.5	1.2	1.0	1.2	1.5	1.5
2014	1.6	1.1	1.5	2.0	2.1	2.1	2.0	1.7	1.7	1.7	1.3	0.8	1.6
2015	-0.1	0.0	-0.1	-0.2	0.0	0.1	0.2	0.2	0.0	0.2	0.5	0.7	0.1
2016	1.4	1.0	0.9	1.1	1.0	1.0	0.8	1.1	1.5	1.6	1.7	2.1	1.3
2017	2.5	2.7	2.4	2.2	1.9	1.6	1.7	1.9	2.2	2.0	2.2	2.1	2.1
2018	2.1	2.2	2.4	2.5	2.8	2.9	2.9	2.7	2.3	2.5	2.2	1.9	2.4
2019	1.6	1.5	1.9	2.0	1.8	1.6	1.8	1.7	1.7	1.8	2.1		

A glance at the chart indicates CPI inflation stands at approximately 2% since 2007. Certainly, that's good news, right? Your money is devaluing much slower than the historical average. However, even a 2% inflation rate can bite into your pension's initial value fairly quickly. For instance, a 2% annual inflation rate eating away for 20 years at a fixed $60K per year annuitized pension would reduce it to $40,378 per year in today's dollars—that's a reduction of almost one-third. Or in other words, in 20 years you would need $89,156 to equal the same purchasing power as $60K today. Either way you slice it, that's not good. If you are interested you can play around with the effect of inflation on your initial pension amount with free online calculators. I have referenced some in the end of chapter resources.

Here's Your COLA, Would You Like A Side of Inflation?

Hopefully, your pension has an inflation-fighting mechanism. By that I mean ideally your pension has a Cost of Living Allowance or Adjustment (COLA) linked to CPI-U for your entire initial payment amount. My High Three U.S. military pension has one, which means the purchasing power of my pension will never erode due to inflation. As you'll see in the next chapter, this makes the process of determining the full value of a pension in today's dollars much easier than a no-COLA pension.

However, starting in 2018, a new pension system called the Blended Retirement System (BRS) came into effect for all new U.S. military recruits. Early drafts of the BRS bill in Congress proposed a COLA calculation of CPI minus 1%, which would have permanently locked in a 1% inflation rate. **It's important to note that CPI minus 1% did not make it into the final version of the BRS, so nobody panic!** Suppose it had though. A 1% inflation rate would have reduced military members' pension values by approximately 22% in 25 years.

Confused as to why a 1% inflation rate compounded over 25 years reduces the value by 22% and **not** 25%? If so, don't feel embarrassed because you're in good company, specifically mine. One of the many proofreaders for this book (let's call him Billy the Kid), who is much better at math than me, caught my error. As Billy explained, "this should be an exponentiation operation, as each year of inflation compounds against the prior year."

Unsure of what exponentiation means and how it works? I was too when I first read the comment. I spent two days hitting my computer with my simian-like hands, screaming *"the files are in the computer"* while trying to understand it. To save you the wasted effort, I recommend you think of inflation's compounding negative effect on the purchasing power of a no-COLA pension as the opposite of compound interest's positive effect on your savings account's interest payments.

Many of us are old enough to remember a time when we could place money into a savings account, and it would earn interest. That's a lot less common since the Great Recession of 2008 and 2009, but humor me, and imagine that we found one. The first interest payment would be based on the initial amount we deposited, known as the principal. But, after the first interest payment, all future interest payments would be calculated using the total of the principal and all previous interest payments. Thus, our interest payments would grow greater over time, as the "interest paid on interest" effect built at an exponential rate.

Inflation's COLA War – and I Don't Mean Coke® vs. Pepsi®

COLA payments for pensions *with* CPI-U linked COLAs experience the same compounding effect. Follow-on COLA payments grow exponentially greater as each new COLA increase compounds on both the original pension amount, plus all previous COLA increases. As a result, each year's new sum forms the *base pay* amount for calculating the following year's COLA payment.

Let me provide an example. Take a pension with a $60K base pay in the first year and a CPI-U linked COLA. At the end of the first year, the COLA increases the base pay by 2% ($60K x .02 = $1200) to keep pace with a 2% inflation rate. As a result, the second year's annual base pay amount would be $61,200. Let's say inflation forces another 2% increase at the end of the second year. That means the COLA increases base pay by $1224 ($61,200 x .02) for a third-year total of $62,424.

As you can see, there's a $24 increase between the second and third-year COLA. The COLA increased by $24 because it compounded using the second year's base pay of $61,200. Interestingly, just like compound interest, this effect starts slow, but builds more rapidly over time, as more COLA increases compound on top of all the previous COLA increases.

A No-COLA Pension's Losing Battle

In contrast, inflation does the opposite to the future purchasing power of a no-COLA pension's fixed annual payment. Since the annual payment never changes, inflation shrinks the future purchasing power of that fixed annual payment more and more each year. In other words, assuming inflation increases annually, a no-COLA pension's annual payment will never be able to purchase more goods than it could in the first year. As a result, to keep pace with inflation's effect, a person living solely on a no-COLA pension's annual income would need to cut their spending by the same amount that inflation increases each year.

Unlike compounding interest though, inflation shrinks future purchasing power more rapidly in the early years than the later years. That means on a year-to-year basis you'd notice the price difference of that aforementioned *Star Wars* movie ticket a lot more between the first and second year of your retirement than between the tenth and eleventh. Or, put another way, which amount would you miss more? The money from scenario number 1 or 2 below?

SCENARIO 1

A 25% decrease in the purchasing power of $1000 between year 1 and 2?

$1000 – $750 = $250

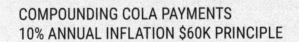

SCENARIO 2

A 25% decrease between year 10 and 11 on the same $1000's purchasing power after 9-years of inflation devaluations?

$107.37 – $85.90 = $21.47

Both of the above values represent a 25% decrease in the previous year's sum, but one value is objectively larger than the other. Why is that? Well, while inflation grows exponentially, it *deflates* purchasing power *fractionally*. Thus, inflation shrinks a bigger purchasing power number into a smaller number in year one and then shrinks it again into an even smaller number the next year.

COMPOUNDING COLA PAYMENTS
10% ANNUAL INFLATION $60K PRINCIPLE

For the graphically minded out there, the difference between the positive effect of compounding COLA payments, and the negative effect of fractional deflation on a no-COLA pension's purchasing power, may be best understood in two charts. For the first example, I made a classic "hockey stick" graph often used to explain compounding interest. In that graph, you can see how an annual increase in COLA increases the nominal (face) value of the pension's annual payment at a compounding rate over time. Please note I used numbers that would help illustrate a point, not ones that I think we'll see anytime soon.

Hopefully, you can see that the gentle slope in the early decades resembles the bottom edge of a hockey stick's shooting face. The steeper part of the curve in the outer decades resembles the shaft of the hockey stick shooting upwards towards the hockey player's hands. The steepness of the curve increases in the outer years due to the compounding effect of the annual 10% COLA increase.

In contrast, if the effect were linear (i.e. the value doubled in the first decade, then quadrupled in the second), the graph would plot in a diagonally straight-line moving up and to the right. But, that's not what happens. The annual payment more than doubles in the first decade, and during the second decade, it increases to 6.7 times as large as the original value. More importantly, by the fortieth year it's 117 times as large as the first year! Again, these are just examples but, hopefully, you get my point.

In the second example (below), the hockey stick graph curves the other way due to inflation's fractional *deflating* effect on the future purchasing power of a no-COLA pension. This means the graph starts with a steep drop in the value of the pension in the early years, but then curves more gently in the later years as the value drops less and less. This is literally what I meant when I said "inflation shrinks future purchasing power more rapidly in the early years than the later years."

COMPOUNDING COLA PAYMENTS
10% ANNUAL INFLATION $60K PRINCIPLE

I believe in mathematical terms the relationship between compounding growth and fractional deflation is called an *inverse* relationship. Keep that in mind for the next chapter because you're going to need it. That said, if my overly long explanation of this *inverted* relationship made you mentally flip me the same *inverted* bird that Maverick flipped the MiG pilot in *Top Gun*, then just hit the Easy Button™. Go to the online inflation calculator link I provide in the end of chapter resources. On that site, you can plug in any fixed-value (e.g. a $60K per year pension), any inflation rate (e.g. 1%), and any number of years (e.g. 25 years) you like, and the calculator will do all that exponentiation stuff for you.

How Common are COLAs?

The results of a completely unscientific poll from my Facebook group showed about one-half of the respondents had a full CPI-linked pension. One-third of respondents had no COLA of any kind. The remainder of respondents had their first $15K linked to a CPI COLA, with the rest subject to inflation—which was the first I had heard of this type of arrangement. One other popular COLA arrangement I've discovered in my research, but not represented by my Facebook respondents, is a flat percentage COLA increase each year, such as 1% or 2%. In some years this may cover all inflation, and in others, it won't. At best a flat percentage slows down inflation's destructive effect, but can't stop it.

Ideally, you now have a better understanding of inflation's impact on the overall value of your pension. As stated previously, I hope everyone's pension has a CPI-linked COLA, but I know that won't always be the case. For those of you with some (or all) of your pension at the mercy of inflation, understand that time is not on your side. The further you progress from the start date of your pension payments, the less purchasing power it represents. Thus, the value of your initial pension amount is a far cry from the value it will hold in your 70s, 80s, or 90s. Your movie ticket gets more expensive, but the amount of money in your pocket stays the same.

Immediacy vs. Inflation

There is one more time-related consideration you must understand when trying to determine the value (or worth) of your pension. It's how quickly pension payments start after retirement. The broad-brush effect is fairly easy to comprehend, but the mathematical details are harder to grasp (again, liberal arts major here!). The gist is that the farther removed your retirement date is from the date when your pension payments start, the less meaningful those payments become.

This is especially true when analyzing the potential success or failure of your investment portfolio's ability to sustain your retirement spending by utilizing a Safe Withdrawal Rate (SWR). For those of you who aren't familiar with the concept of a SWR, it's essentially the percentage of your investment portfolio (i.e. your nest egg) that you can safely withdraw each year, no matter the market conditions, without running out of money in the portfolio. The original SWR is better known as the 4% Rule, but it's not a rule, it's more like a rule of thumb.

A Safe Withdrawal Rate Segue

The 4% Rule (of thumb) was developed by the financial planner Bill Bengen in the 1990s. He discovered it after analyzing 30-year rolling stock market returns from the Great Depression through the mid-1980s. In doing so he determined that hypothetical retirees, who invested in 50% stocks and 50% bonds over this period, could have withdrawn up to 4.15% from their investments annually without running out of money.

You read that correctly. Even in scenarios where withdrawals started during the worst economic conditions the U.S. ever faced (aka the Great Depression), Bengen's model worked. So, as you can see, understanding SWRs is vital if you intend to retire and live, at least partially, on the proceeds from your investments. If this is a first heard concept for you, I suggest you check out the additional references linked at the end of this chapter.

Back to the Impact of Pension Immediacy

Part of the explanation for the pension immediacy phenomenon is due to inflation, which, after our *Star Wars* discussion, I hope you now understand. Let's say you retire at 55 and lock in an initial pension payment amount of $3,000 a month. However, let's also say your pension payments do not start until age 62 (which is a fairly common feature in some sectors). What happens if the pension doesn't have a

CPI-linked COLA, or some other ability to grow with inflation? Well, that equals seven years of inflation-linked devaluation against your pension payments before you ever receive a dime.

At a 3% historical inflation average, that equals 18.7% of your pension gone (there's that *exponentiation* thing again) before you ever get to use it. This means, for comparison's sake, your future pension's monthly payment at age 62 would only purchase $2,439 (81.3%) worth of age 55's goods. Now maybe that's a lot of your planned monthly retirement budget, or maybe that's a little, but no matter what, I bet it would hurt.

A situation like this makes that pension less meaningful to you and probably makes you more reliant on other income streams like withdrawals from your investment portfolio. Unfortunately, a heavier reliance on other income streams doesn't come without risk. For instance, suppose you retire before your pension payments start, and in the meantime, you intend to rely on withdrawals from your investments. If your investment portfolio's value drops significantly at the beginning of that early retirement, then you might run into a scenario known as Sequence of Returns Risk. This means there's a possibility your portfolio may run out of money even if you utilize a Safe Withdrawal Rate (SWR), and it won't be able to provide that steady stream of money you planned on until pension payments start. Couple that scenario to the inflation-linked devaluation of a no-COLA pension, and the situation could hurt even worse.

Of course, the solution to that problem is to increase your initial payment amount in line with inflation, like with a CPI-linked COLA. This mitigates the inflation-linked portion of the immediacy problem. In the above scenario that means your pension payments retain the same purchasing power as the day you retired, even if your payments do not start for seven years, because they will increase by 18.7% (i.e. your $3,000 monthly payment is now $3,689).

The problem is that a CPI-linked COLA is typically something that your employer decides to offer. It is not something you typically get to negotiate. So, *if* you find yourself in a pension program without an inflation-linked COLA, and *if* your payments don't start immediately, then (again) understand that time is your enemy. Not only that, but understand that your pension is not worth nearly as much as a full-COLA pension. At the very least, you should ensure that you devalue the impact of that pension accordingly when making your *worth vs. worth* it determination. Alternatively, you could always try to build a COLA yourself. If that idea interests you, there is more information below.

Build Your Own COLA

A reader of mine developed the idea of a Do It Yourself (DIY) Cost of Living Adjustment (COLA) because his pension did not have one. He asked me if I could determine the amount of money he should save and invest to build a DIY COLA for a $50K per year pension. Since I'm not a polymath, I contacted FI blogging and math superstar Big ERN (Karsten) from the Early Retirement Now blog. Together we came up with some rough order of magnitude projections for 40-year and 60-year retirement scenarios.

Using an estimated 2% annual inflation rate (and therefore a 2% annual withdrawal rate), we determined my reader would need to save anywhere between $430,000 for a 40-year DIY COLA to $570,000 for a 60-year DIY COLA on his $50K per year pension. Also, my reader would need to invest those amounts with an 80/20 stock-to-bond mix on the first day of retirement to ensure that he wouldn't run out of money prematurely. We've documented this case study online and it's listed on the end of the chapter resources page.

The Immediacy Effect

There is another aspect to this immediacy phenomenon that a CPI-linked COLA doesn't mitigate. For lack of a better term, I call it the *Immediacy Effect*. Unfortunately, I don't understand the math to explain it well. However, I know someone who does, and that's Big ERN McCracken (aka Karsten) at Early Retirement Now (ERN). It was his article that clued me in to the *Immediacy Effect* in the first place. What I learned from his article is this: the further from your retirement point that your pension payments begin, the less positive of an impact the payments will have on your employment of a Safe Withdrawal Rate (SWR) from your investment portfolio.

Thus, **you need to exercise spending caution in the retirement period before your pension payments start.** In other words, based on the funky effects of compounding rates of return, the time value of money, and some other math-related stuff **don't overspend early in retirement when your pension isn't paying out.** You may be tempted to think that your later-starting pension payments will repair the earlier damage done to your investment portfolio by over withdrawing, but unfortunately, the math doesn't work that way.

Testing the Immediacy Effect

I can attest that the *Immediacy Effect* plays out in my retirement calculations. Based on my research, I concluded that it's prudent to plan for a 25% reduction in Social Security benefits if your full payments start after 2034. My full payments are projected to start in 2042.

A 25% reduction takes my estimated full payment of $14.5K per year (p/y) down to $10.9K p/y. That's a $3,600 p/y difference. Intuitively, it seems like that reduction should have a huge impact on the probability of success (i.e. the probability that I don't run out of money) for my retirement spending plan. Yet, when I re-ran my early retirement calculations in my preferred retirement calculator (Flexible Retirement Planner) with a 25% reduced Social Security payment, guess how much the reduction impacted the probability of success for my overall retirement plan? One... whole... percent.

That's right, a 25% reduced Social Security payment that starts 22-years after my proposed early retirement date, reduced my retirement spend plan's probability of success from 99% to 98%. That's barely any impact at all. On the other hand, if I reduce my estimated pension payments (which start immediately after retirement) by that same $3,600 (from $50.3K p/y to $46.7K p/y), and run that same simulation, it reduces my chances of success from 99% to 92%. That's a far bigger statistical impact, which I can only explain through the *Immediacy Effect*.

—

Interested in more resources that explain inflation, COLAs, SWRs, and Sequence of Return Risk (SRR)? Check out the Chapter 8 resources at: https://grumpusmaximus.com/golden-albatross-book-chapter-resources/chapter-8/

Valuing Different Types of Pensions

For the long chapters in this book, I've included an end of chapter takeaway section to refresh you on all the topics covered. After reading this chapter, you should now understand the three fundamental inputs to consider when determining the worth (i.e. value) side of the *worth vs. worth it* equation. Those inputs are (1) your pension's Initial Dollar Value (IDV), (2) your pension's interaction with inflation, and (3) your pension's interaction with the Immediacy Effect. It's also worth noting that:

■ Not all pensions are created equal! More valuable pensions carry certain features that less valuable pensions do not. Most notably they:

‒ Vest workers after shorter periods on the job

‒ Calculate IDV using formulas with high-income averages and percentage multipliers like this one:

» $[(A+B+C)/3] \times .66$ = Initial yearly pension with 2% bump in the multiple for each year of service over 25 years; maximum of 100%

‒ Provide a CPI-linked COLA for the entire pension amount, like my military pension

‒ Start payouts immediately upon retirement, again, like my military pension

■ The purchasing power of a pension with an inflation-linked COLA never changes over time, since the COLA increases base pay to keep up with inflation

‒ Meaning, as your movie ticket price increases year over year, the money in your pocket increases by the same percentage as the ticket

■ The opposite can be said of a pension with no COLA. Assuming inflation always goes up, you can never purchase the same amount of goods as you did in the first year

‒ Meaning, you go to the movie and the ticket price increases, but the amount of money in your pocket stays the same

■ Not everyone is fortunate enough to work a job with access to a pension that meets all of the above criteria. The less a pension resembles the above points, the less it's objectively worth in retirement.

‒ How that impacts your *worth vs. worth it* decision will come down to your circumstances

Chapter 9

How to Determine Your Pension's Total Dollar Value (TDV)

Determining Total Dollar Value (TDV)

Initial Dollar Value (IDV) doesn't tell the whole story regarding your pension's future worth. Depending on your pension's features, IDV may prove drastically different than your pension's Total Dollar Value (TDV). Thus, it's vitally important for someone caught in the maw of the *Golden Albatross* to take what they learned when calculating IDV, and apply it when determining their pension's TDV.

I originally intended to write about good pension calculators found on the web that could help you place a TDV on your pension. But, it turns out that most generic pension calculators on the web stink...if you can find one at all. It also turns out that most pension plans have their own calculators.

In hindsight that makes sense because, as we discussed in Chapter 8, each pension plan has its own formula to calculate IDV. However, the existence of a calculator on your pension fund's website doesn't decrease the importance of determining the TDV of your pension by hand. This is especially true when making your *worth vs. worth it* decision. After all, you want to ensure those numbers and calculations are correct, don't you? That said, I can also list several great reasons for determining your pension's TDV outside of the *Golden Albatross* decision cycle.

Good Lookin' Out

The most important reason for calculating your pension's TDV is to ensure your Human Resources (HR) and/or pay department give you what you're entitled to upon retirement. This may seem like obvious advice, but I'm not so sure. The Department of Labor's (DOL's) Employee Benefits Security Administration (EBSA), the U.S federal office designed to protect employees' retirement benefits, has a web page with the *10 Common Causes of Errors in Pension Calculation*. It's worth a read, especially since 2 of the 10 most common errors are due to simple math. I doubt the EBSA would waste time stating the obvious in a list of ten common errors if it weren't happening, so make sure your administrators are doing the basic math correctly.

It so happens that I have a pension administrator in my *Golden Albatross* Facebook Group. After I sent Michelle the above-mentioned link, she advised:

> ...*I would definitely recommend that everyone...do their own basic pension calculation. I've had very few people I've worked with over the years do this...Our process is to have our outside administrator do the calculation...we also independently do the calculation before we review theirs. The idea being that it's unlikely both will make the same error, so if we match, we're good to go. If not, we investigate until we find the error. This has worked well for me...Still, while this makes me confident that we're providing accurate calculations, I think everyone should understand their own calculation and be able to challenge it if they're not confident in the accuracy.*

I think that's great advice, especially since I doubt everyone's organization has someone as conscientious as Michelle looking out for their best interest. Also, I presume it's hard, if not impossible, to fix an error in your pension calculation after you've retired, signed all the paperwork, and started to receive checks. By doing the math yourself, you'll save yourself the headache, if not the heart attack.

Two Heads are Better Than One (and Legally Required)

The second reason why it's important to determine a TDV for your pension is the issue of survivorship. If you're married or have children, then by U.S. law your pension plan must offer some sort of survivorship plan. Survivorship essentially acts as an insurance policy, allowing you to nominate a certain percentage of your pension to pass to your spouse and/or minor children when you die. In turn, this reduces the total monthly payment to you while living (akin to a monthly premium).

Consequently, if you don't know the TDV of your pension, you'll have no idea if electing the survivorship benefit connected to your pension is a good value. Who knows? You might be able to find a better value through something like term life insurance, but without knowing your pension's TDV, you won't be able to compare the two options.

It's important to note that comparing term insurance to the survivorship option in your pension isn't necessarily an apples to apples comparison. If your pension has a COLA, then inflation makes the survivorship option a lot more cost-effective.

Survivorship...

...is something that must be offered by U.S. law to a pensioner upon his or her retirement. The premiums for survivorship are determined by the percentage of the pension that a pensioner elects to pass onto a spouse or minor age children upon death. These premiums reduce a pensioner's monthly income accordingly. Depending on the pension plan there may be some tax-advantaged status for the payments. This is a BIG decision; survivorship premiums typically aren't cheap.

There are some obvious reasons why a couple (per U.S. law, if married, it must be both spouses' decision) may choose to either elect or decline survivorship. Lack of family, plenty of retirement assets, major health problems for the pensioner, and/or a significant amount of previously purchased life insurance are just some of the factors that would make a survivorship decision relatively easy.

Much like other retirement decisions though, there is a wrong answer. That would be if you don't elect survivorship, but it turns out your survivors needed it. Of course, you won't be around to see if you made the correct decision! I've included more details in the end of chapter resources with useful methods to compare costs with term insurance.

And Finally!

Lump Sums are the third reason why it's important to calculate a TDV for your pension regardless of the *Golden Albatross* decision cycle. Many pension plans these days, including public pensions, offer the opportunity to take some, or all, of your future pension's value in a lump-sum payment immediately upon retirement.

As explained in Chapter 7, pension funds offer lump sums to transfer the risk associated with the uncertain future financial liability of the retiree's annuity to the retiree. Or in plain English, pension funds offer lump sums because retirees may live longer than planned, and the fund may run out of money to pay them. This means it's cheaper to pay a pensioner an estimated lump-sum value for their future pension in the present, to decrease or eliminate the liability of paying them (and their survivors) a larger amount of money spread out over the remainder of their lives.

Now, there might be a good reason for you to take a lump sum but without knowing your pension's TDV, you'd have no idea just how much money the pension plan stands to save (and you stand to lose) from the lump-sum offer. I discuss this issue more in Chapter 10.

Inflation-Paced Calculations

No matter the reason for calculating TDV, let's see if we can do it. As you will recall from the previous chapter, the first thing we must do is calculate IDV, which is based on your pension's formula. Since different pension systems have different pension formulas, it's best to check your pension's website or annual literature to find out what yours is.

While on the website, you will hopefully find a calculator that will at least calculate the IDV for you. If not, go back to the previous chapter and review how to draft a mathematical formula to do it yourself. Even if you find a calculator, you may still want to make the calculations by hand...just to be safe. You may also want to cross-reference your result to someone else's who worked a similar length of time at your workplace. This is *your* pension, after all. No one besides you and your family has more of a vested interest in ensuring the calculations are correct.

Grumpus's Pre-Tax Pension Calculator

YEARS OUT	YEAR	MONTHLY PAY	ANNUAL PAY	CUMULATIVE
1	2020	**$4,731.54**	**$56,778.47**	$56,778.47
10	2029	$5,699.22	$68,390.66	$624,254.36
20	2039	$7,011.21	$84,134.48	$1,392,050.44
30	2049	$8,625.41	$103,504.90	$2,336,655.14
40	2059	$10,611.25	$127,335.04	**$3,498,696.08**

When you calculated your IDV, did it come out in a monthly or yearly amount? The U.S. military's pension calculator spits out results like the chart above. It provides monthly and annual values, as highlighted by the **underlined bold text** in columns three and four in the chart. If your calculator only provides a monthly amount, go ahead and calculate the annual amount since we'll need it for our calculations below. Ignore the rest of my chart for now; I'll refer back to it as needed.

If you are one of the lucky ones I described in the previous chapter, whose pension starts immediately upon retirement and has a COLA linked to inflation as listed in the Consumer Price Index (CPI), then your task is simple. You can calculate TDV in today's dollars by multiplying the yearly total for your IDV by your Estimated Life Span (ELS). I find that the Social Security Administration retains the most accurate life span data for the U.S., and they have a handy little calculator that will display it for you based on your current age and gender. However, you can get your lifespan estimate from a lot of different places including looking at your family tree.

So, what does the formula for the TDV of a pension with a full inflation-linked COLA look like? It's fairly simple because in mathematical terms it looks like:

$$TDV = IDV \times \text{Expected Life Span (ELS)}$$

So, if I were to take the annual amount highlighted in the **underlined bold text** above ($56,778.47) and multiply it by 40 (putting me at the ripe old age of 85) my TDV in today's dollars would be $2,271,138.80.

$$\$2{,}271{,}138.80 = \$56{,}778.47 \times (\,40\,)$$

Notice that my TDV sum is a different amount than the cumulative value (**$3,498,696.08**) calculated in bold in the lower right-hand corner of the chart above. Why? Well, an inflation-linked COLA is built into the military pension calculator, so the payments increase by some nominal amount representing inflation every year. The calculator doesn't tell me what value is used for inflation, but it doesn't matter.

Since my pension payments will keep pace with inflation, it essentially eliminates the need to consider inflation's effect. And since my pension starts immediately, I don't need to discount it for the immediacy effect either. Thus, in any circumstance where a person has a pension with CPI-linked COLA that starts immediately upon retirement, IDV multiplied by your ELS equals TDV.

Non-Inflation or Partial Inflation Paced Calculations

For no-COLA pensioners and pensioners with some sort of flat rate COLA, I hope that your pension's website has a calculator that does all this for you. If not, get ready to roll up your sleeves and make some calculations that are a little more complicated than the simple multiplication from the previous section. That said, even if your pension's website provides a calculator, it's in your best interest to run the numbers manually just to be sure. Remember that list of ten pension calculation mistakes I referred to earlier!

Don't freak out if your math skills aren't the best because I'm not going to force you to come up with any formulas on your own. Besides, you're more prepared than you think. My long-winded (but chart-filled) Chapter 8 deep dive into inflation's inverted impact on no-COLA pensions comes full-circle in this chapter.

At most, all you'll need to do is plug numbers into a formula that Billy the Kid (the proofreader I mentioned in the last chapter) pointed me towards. It's a formula that I thoroughly tested and I believe it is superior to one I previously used on my blog. So much so, that I updated all my blog articles that used my old formula, and sent emails to anyone who previously asked me to calculate their no-COLA pension's TDV. As a result, I'm confident this formula provides the type of value we're looking for, but with a much greater degree of accuracy than anything I could've devised on my own.

Before we dive head-first into the formula though, I want to ensure you understand what we're attempting to calculate. Doing so will help you understand the formula that much better. So here it goes...we are calculating **the cumulative value of your no-COLA pension payments in retirement while taking into account the cumulative negative effect of inflation on that value.** In other words, due to inflation, we are *deflating* the future sum of all payments into the equivalent purchasing power of retirement year one's dollars.

Crucially, this formula captures inflation's negative effect on an annual basis. The formula must do this because, as I discussed in Chapter 8 when *deflating* future values into present dollars, inflation works at a negative fractional rate. This means each year's sum of pension payments is different than the previous year because inflation's negative effect builds on the previous year's value. As Billy explained it to me:

> *In reality, what is needed to figure out this value is much more akin to calculating the future value of an investment with regular contributions coming into a portfolio, where the growth rate is simply negative [due to] inflation.*

Remember the hockey stick curve from Chapter 8 of the no-COLA pension that started steep on the left but curved more gently the further it moved to the right? If not, I placed it on page 111 for reference. In Chapter 8, I used the chart to discuss the difference between the purchasing power of a no-COLA pension's first annual pension payment ($60K) versus various points in the future, like 20 years ($8,918).

To calculate the TDV of a no-COLA pension though, we need to do something different. We need to capture the sum of each year's inflation-adjusted payments as they plot along the curve, and then add them all together. This formula will do that.

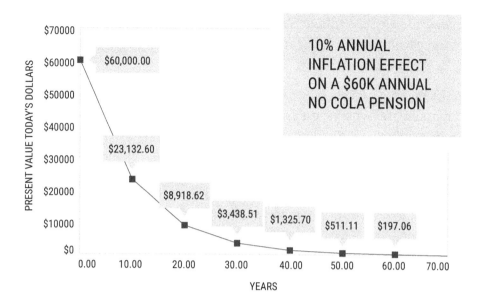

$70000

$60000 $60,000.00

$50000

PRESENT VALUE TODAY'S DOLLARS

$40000

$30000 $23,132.60

$20000

$10000 $8,918.62

$3,438.51 $1,325.70 $511.11 $197.06

$0

0.00   10.00   20.00   30.00   40.00   50.00   60.00   70.00

YEARS

10% ANNUAL INFLATION EFFECT ON A $60K ANNUAL NO COLA PENSION

Enough Talk, Just Get to the Damn Equation!

I agree, so here it is:

> * No COLA Pension TDV = IDV [((1−r) ^ (ELS+1) − (1−r)) /−r]
>
> IDV = annual pension payments
> r = annual inflation rate (negative growth)
> ELS = Expected Life Span (or any number of years you want to use)

*Note: this formula starts inflation with the first year's payment, which essentially means your pension payment devalues throughout the first year, in real-time. In my opinion, this is the more accurate way to calculate inflation's effect since real-world inflation's effect doesn't wait until the end of the year to impact your household budget for staples like food.

For the math lovers out there, who think this formula looks vaguely familiar, it's a modified equation for investment growth with regular contributions, like the one below. However, the TDV formula above drops the initial principal represented by "P" in the below formula, since there is none. The no-COLA TDV formula above also switches out "c" for the IDV acronym that I like to use. Finally, the formula above turns the growth rate, represented by (r), below, negative to simulate inflation.

$$\text{Balance} = P(1+r)^{\wedge}Y + c[((1+r)^{\wedge}(Y+1)-(1+r))/r]$$

P = Initial principal (not used in the TDV equation)
r = growth rate
Y = Years of compounding (what I called ELS above)
c = regular contributions

Or, as Billy related:

> The equation ... is basically the same equation as a compounded growth of [an] investment with periodic regular contributions, though in this case, the growth rate is inverted (inflation) and the contributions into the portfolio are ... the pension's payments.

There's my favorite *Top Gun* reference again: *inverted!* I was hoping it would make an appearance somehow. Jokes aside though, what Billy told us is what I essentially said above. The formula captures each year's pension payment, devalues it according to the cumulative inflation rate, and adds that sum to all the other ones to obtain one overall inflation-adjusted sum.

To prevent all the non-math loving heads (like mine) from exploding while looking at the above formula, I plugged some numbers into the equation below as a practical example. To compare my result below to the full COLA pension calculation from two-sections ago, I used the same $56,778.47 as the annual payment (IDV). I also used the same 40-year ELS from above. Unlike the full COLA example though, I had to select an inflation rate. I chose 2% since it's the U.S. Federal Reserve's target rate.

Finally, I translated everything into Microsoft Excel syntax to make the calculation run on a spreadsheet. As a result, you can copy everything below starting with the "=" symbol and continuing to the right, plop it into your electronic spreadsheet of choice, and play around with it. When you do, what you'll get is a result like this:

$$\text{No-COLA Pension TDV} =$$
$$56778.47 * (((\ 1 - .02\ )\ \char94\ (\ 40 + 1\ ) - (\ 1 - .02\ ))\ /\ -\ .02\ )$$

$$\text{No-COLA Pension TDV} =$$
$$\mathbf{\$1,542,141.87}$$

A TDV of **$1,542,141.87** is a significantly smaller amount than the $2,271,138.80 TDV for the full COLA pension from earlier in this chapter. In fact, it's 32% smaller. Such is the power of inflation, specifically inflation's inverted effect on purchasing power. This is the reason why I covered it so extensively in the last chapter.

A word of caution though, assuming the inflation rate is accurate: **$1,542,141.87** represents a no-COLA pension's TDV in first retirement year dollars. If your retirement is still years off, you'll need to deflate this value even further to put that value into today's dollars. I'll show you how to do that below in the *Delayed Pension Payout* section. In the meantime, keep in mind that TDV has several handy uses, such as a comparison tool for lump-sum offers, which I cover in Chapter 10.

What are some other tips I can give you? If your pension has a COLA that is linked only partially to CPI, or some other method, like a flat rate COLA increase of 1% or 2% per year, then you need to modify your inflation rate accordingly. For instance, in the previous chapter, I pointed out that one proposal for the latest military retirement system in the U.S. (**which fortunately didn't make the final draft**) intended an annual COLA that would've been minus 1% of CPI. This essentially would've subjected future pension payments under this system to a 1% inflation rate in perpetuity.

Thus, if I were to calculate the TDV of that annual $56,778.47 pension using a 1% inflation rate over 40 years, it would equal a **$1,860,732.43** TDV in year one dollars. Again, that's a lot less than the $2.271 million in my CPI-linked COLA pension scenario. In fact, it's approximately 18% less. On the other hand, it's 17% more than the 2% inflation-adjusted TDV of $1,542,141.87 in my no-COLA pension scenario above. Under certain circumstances, the **$1.86 million** TDV can be used to compare to a lump-sum offer your pension fund might offer. However, there are several caveats, which is why I discuss this further in Chapter 10.

Shortcuts and Tools

For argument's sake, let's say you have a *friend* whose math skills suck. As a result, even plugging numbers into a formula like the one above is a challenge. Maybe some of the mathematical symbols used in the above formula, like the little up arrow (i.e. ^), have him confused. Or, maybe she simply forgot the rules of her mathematical order of operations. As a result, this *friend* is looking for an Easy Button™ solution for calculating TDV for a no-COLA pension.

Well, if you had a math-challenged *friend* like me ... errr ... I mean if you had a math-challenged *friend* like *that*, then I'd point him or her to one of two websites, depending on their preference. For the simplest solution, your *friend* could go to Buyupside.com's *Growing Annuity Due Calculator - Future Value* page. Once there, they should do the following:

1. Enter the annual pension amount (e.g. $56,778.47) into the "Payment" box

2. Enter the projected annual inflation rate as a negative number (e.g. -2) in the "Discount Rate" box

3. Leave a zero as the "Payment Growth Rate"

4. Enter the projected ELS in years (e.g. 40) in the "Number Payments" box

5. Hit the "Calculate" button

6. When the grey "The following error(s) occurred: - rate must contain a number between 1 and 100" error box appears, hit "OK", and then ignore it

7. Look at the "Future Value" box and obtain your TDV (e.g. $1,542,141.87)

Pretty cool, huh? If you're wondering why this hack works, then read the "Computational Notes" section below the calculator on the web page. When you do, you'll see that the first formula listed looks a lot, but not exactly, like the formula Billy the Kid pointed me towards.

However, entering a zero in the "Payment Growth Rate" box, and a negative value in the "Discount Rate" box, essentially turns the Buyupside.com formula into the same formula that Billy gave me.

I'm just happy the calculator still computes the value even though the error box appears. I say that because during research for this chapter, I looked at a lot of websites with calculators for various financial situations, and only found one other where these hacks worked.

Speaking of which, if your *friend* wants the more elegant Easy Button™ solution, with more settings and no error box, then they can go to Omnicalculator.com's *Future Value of Annuity Calculator*. A user must still set the "Interest Rate" to a negative number to simulate inflation (e.g. -2). However, this calculator provides more input options than the Buyupside.com calculator. As a result, a user can play around more easily with some of the different variables that impact TDV and see what happens.

For example, toggling between the "Ordinary Annuity" and "Annuity Due" settings in the "Type of Annuity" section on the Omnicalculator allows a user to move the simulated inflation calculation from the end to the beginning (respectively) of the chosen "Compounding Period". The tool defaults to the "Ordinary Annuity" (i.e. the end of the "Compounding Period") setting. So, when I input all the same variables as before (e.g. a $56.7K pension, 40-year ELS, and 2% inflation rate) I must toggle the setting to "Annuity Due" just to get the same results as the Billy the Kid supplied formula (e.g. $1,542,141.87). If I don't, then the calculated TDV is $1,573,614.15. That's a $31,472.28 difference in TDV just by moving the timing of my simulated inflation calculations!

Delayed Payout Pensions: Scenario 1

About the only pension TDV scenario I haven't discussed is that of the delayed pension payout. This is the type of pension that is vulnerable to the *Immediacy Effect*, which Big ERN discovered, and I described in the previous chapter. Since there are numerous permutations of pensions that start years after a person retires, I'll stick with the two most common: (1) a no-COLA pension whose payments start at some point in the future, but is subject to inflation over its entire lifespan, and (2) a delayed pension whose COLA only starts when the actual payments start. If you have a pension that does something slightly different, you'll have to modify the techniques I show you below to suit your situation.

For these two scenarios, let's keep all the previous values the same (i.e. inflation rate, annual pension amount, and ELS). However, let's add the fact that you're 55 years old but your annual $56,778.47 pension doesn't start until age 62. Now, maybe you're retiring at 55 and have to wait until 62 for your pension to payout. Alternatively, you might be 55 now and just curious as to what your pension's TDV will be in today's dollars, rather than 62 when you retire and payments start. Either way, there's a seven-year offset from the present until your pension starts. Just as important, you already know the pension's first-year payment, or Initial Dollar Value (IDV), will be $56,778.47, which won't change between now and then. Finally, you think you'll live 40 more years after payments start, and you believe the average annual inflation rate over the entire 47-year time frame will be 2%.

With those parameters set, let's tackle the *no-COLA over the entire lifespan of the pension* scenario first. How should we calculate TDV in this case? We must account for 47 years' worth of inflation, not all of which include payments. The first seven years of inflation eats away at the value of the annual pension payments before they even start. On the other hand, the following 40 years of inflation coincide with payments.

Simply put, there are two ways to tackle this TDV calculation. You either account for the 40 years (age 62 to 102) first and the seven years (age 55 to 62) second. Or, vice versa. Both methods produce the same results if you're consistent.

As you'll see from the first set of calculations below, I started with the 40 years (age 62 to 102) first. This means for Step 1, I ran the numbers through the same no-COLA Pension TDV formula that I used in the above sections of this chapter (i.e. Billy the Kid's formula). By doing this I obtained the inflation-adjusted TDV for the 40-years' worth of pension payments between ages 62 and 102. Once again, I wrote all formulas in Excel syntax, so you could copy everything from the equals sign rightwards into a spreadsheet if desired:

STEP 1

Age 62 No-COLA Pension TDV =
$$56778.47 * (((\ 1 - .02\ )\ ^\wedge\ (\ 40 + 1\ ) - (\ 1 - .02\ ))\ /\ - .02\ )$$

Age 62 No-COLA Pension TDV =
$1,542,141.87

For Step 2, I further reduced that 40-year TDV to account for inflation's negative effect over the 7-year gap between ages 55 and 62. In this case, I used a standard Present Value (PV) formula to devalue the sum from Step 1. I could do this because I only needed to account for inflation's seven-year cumulative effect on that total. With no pension payments to account for during the seven-year time-frame, there was no need for a more complicated formula like the one above. My step 2 calculations are on the next page:

STEP 2

Present Value (PV) formula =
amount / (1 + inflation rate) ^ number years

Age 55 Present Value (PV) formula =
1542141.87 / (1 + .02) ^ 7

Age 55 TDV = $1,342,527.30

Thus, for this method (i.e. tackling the 40-year timeframe first) the TDV for a no-COLA pension that starts seven years from now equals **$1,342,527.30**. That said, there's no reason why you couldn't use some Easy Button™ calculators to do this work. Start with either Buyupside's *Growing Annuity* or the Omnicalculator's *Future Value of Annuity* calculator that I referred to earlier in the chapter. Then move to Buyupside's *Inflation Calculator*. Either way, manual or calculator assisted, the TDV for the pension at age 55 is **$1,342,527.30**.

The next question to answer is this: if I step through the calculations in reverse order, do I still get the same result? In other words, if I devalue the annual $56,778.47 payment over seven years of inflation first, and then run that value through our no-COLA TDV formula for the following 40-year period, will I still get a TDV for the 47 years that's **$1,342,527.30**? Let's find out.

For Step 1 below, I ran the $56,778.47 value through the same PV formula as above to simulate seven-years' worth of inflation on that value. Then, for Step 2, I crunched the reduced annual payment value through Billy the Kid's supplied no-COLA TDV formula. As a result, my formulas looked like this:

STEP 1

Present Value (PV) formula =
amount / (1 + inflation rate) ^ number years

Age 55 to 62 Present Value (PV) formula =
56778.47 / (1 + .02) ^ 7

Age 55 to 62 Present Value (PV) formula = $49,429.075

STEP 2

No-COLA Pension TDV =
49429.075 * (((1 − .02) ^ (40 + 1) - (1 − .02)) / − .02)

Age 62 No-COLA Pension TDV = **$1,342,527.30**

Wow, it worked! Not only that but if you use the Easy Button™ calculators, they give you the same value. Hopefully, those results reassure you that I'm not trying to feed you a line of B.S. If nothing else, I'm reassured knowing that I'm not feeding you a line of B.S.

Illustration: You'll have to use this one day...

Delayed Payout Pensions: Scenario 2

Some delayed pensions are subject to inflation from the point of retirement (e.g. age 55) until pension payments start (e.g. age 62). In other words, that seven-year gap from Scenario 1. However, unlike Scenario 1, once pension payments start, so too does a full COLA. Thus, inflation is negated for the remainder of retirement (e.g. the 40-year ELS).

If that's your situation, then you must make yet another two-step calculation. Your first calculation should simply account for inflation's negative effect on your pension's projected annual payment over the gap period. You can do this by using the PV formula from page 120.

For Step 2, instead of using the no-COLA TDV formula from page 120, replace it with the simpler full inflation-linked COLA TDV formula I provided in the first part of this chapter. You're permitted to use the simpler formula because the full inflation-linked COLA, that starts with your pension payments, negates all future effects of inflation. Thus, you can ignore inflation for the remainder of your calculations.

Again, using all the basic parameters from the previous scenario like a 2% inflation rate, the TDV calculations for an annual $56,778.47 pension that starts seven years into the future with a full COLA, would look like this:

STEP 1

Present Value (PV) formula =
amount / (1 + inflation rate) ^ number years

Age 55 to 62 Present Value (PV) formula = 56778.47 / (1 + .02) ^ 7

Age 55 to 62 Present Value (PV) formula = 49429.075

IDV = $49,429.075

STEP 2

Full COLA Pension TDV = IDV * Expected Life Span (ELS)

Age 62 to 102 full COLA Pension TDV =
49429.075*40

7-year delayed pension with 40-year full COLA TDV =
$1,977,163.00

Right then, the TDV for a seven-year delayed pension with a 40-year full COLA is **$1,977,163**. That makes sense when you think about it. Assuming you're still awake, and that you can remember the beginning of this extremely long chapter, then you may recall the TDV calculation I made for my full COLA pension which started immediately with a $56,778.47 annual pension. In case you can't remember that many words ago, the TDV was $2,271,138.80 for a 40-year ELS.

Coincidentally, the above 47-year calculation also contains a full COLA pension paying out over 40-years. It too negates inflation's effect. However, unlike my full COLA immediate payout pension, the above pension is subject to seven years of devaluation by a 2% inflation rate before full COLA pension payments kick in. Thus, we should have expected a smaller TDV than my pension.

On the other hand, we also should have expected a much larger TDV for delayed pension payout Scenario 2 than Scenario 1 since the majority of inflation's negative effects are mitigated by the COLA that starts with pension payments—which is exactly what we got. Remember though, these are just examples built on the two most common types of delayed pensions. Your pension may do something a bit different, which is why I recommend anyone with a pension offset by a significant chunk of time to do the research themselves.

Familiarizing yourself with your pension's specific details is always a good thing. I say that because based on my research into pensions, I've come to believe that every DBP is unique. This means once you've studied one DBP, you've still only studied one DBP.

Interested in more resources that explain inflation, COLAs, SWRs, and Sequence of Return Risk (SRR)? Check out the Chapter 8 resources at: https://grumpusmaximus.com/golden-albatross-book-chapter-resources/chapter-8/

Well, that wraps up the different methods I've devised to calculate a pension's Total Dollar Value (TDV). In no way do I think this is a definitive list. On the other hand, I believe the methods I demonstrated cover the majority of pension situations. Hopefully, I haven't lost you. Verbally explaining math is hard and this chapter wasn't concise! Still, this chapter is one of the most important in the book, so it's imperative you understand which formula applies to your pension situation. As a result, let's do a quick review of what I covered:

- Calculating Total Dollar Value (TDV) is crucial for the *Golden Albatross* decision, but has other uses as well, like deciding on Survivorship payments

- Calculating TDV for full inflation-linked COLA pensions is the easiest calculation since you can effectively ignore inflation
  - You simply take your Expected Life Span (ELS) and multiply it by the Initial Dollar Value (IDV) of your pension
  - The equation is: TDV = IDV * ELS

- Calculating the TDV for no-COLA pensions (or pensions that lock in a certain inflation rate) is much harder. The equation looks like this:
  - No-COLA Pension TDV = $IDV(((1-r)^{(ELS+1)}-(1-r))/-r)$
  - Where:
    - » IDV = annual pension payments
    - » r = annual inflation rate (negative growth)
    - » ELS = Expected Life Span (or any number of years you want to use)
  - Remember! This formula makes the inflation calculation on the front end of the time-period (annually in the examples I showed you) as opposed to waiting until the end of the time-period

- Alternatively, two online calculators can make the no-COLA TDV calculations for you, if you hack them with negative values for growth to represent inflation
  - See the online resources at the end of the chapter for more details

- Delayed payout pension TDV calculations are the most complicated TDV calculations to make because there are many types of delayed payout pensions, and each calculation requires multiple steps. I showed you how to calculate the TDV for the two most common delayed pension payout scenarios:

- Scenario 1: Delayed payout pension with no COLA
- Scenario 2: Delayed payout pension with a full COLA that only starts once pension payments start

- In both scenarios, I assumed that I knew my IDV already (e.g. $56,778.47) and that it was not going to change between age 55 retirement and the start of payments at 62 (i.e. the delay period)
- Thus, in both scenarios you can use a Present Value (PV) formula to deflate the pension's IDV (e.g. $56,778.47) over the delay period (e.g. seven-years) as Step 1:
  - » PV formula = amount/(1 + inflation rate)^number years
  - » Age 55 to 62 Present Value (PV) formula =56778.47/(1+.02)^7
  - » Age 55 to 62 Present Value (PV) formula = $49,429.075

- Step 2 actions depended on the delayed pension scenario:
- Scenario 1: No COLA throughout the entire retirement (e.g. 47 years)
  - » Take the PV sum (e.g. $49,429.075) and run it through the no- COLA Pension TDV formula
  - » No-COLA Pension TDV =49429.075*(((1-.02)^(40+1)-(1-.02))/-.02)
  - » Delayed no-COLA Pension TDV = $1,342,527.30
  - » You can run the scenario in the opposite direction. To do so, devalue the 40 years first, then devalue for the 7-year gap

- Scenario 2: Full COLA once payments start after the delay
  - » Take the PV sum (e.g. $49,429.075) and run it through the less complicated TDV equation for full-COLA pensions
  - » TDV = IDV * Expected Life Span (ELS)
  - » Age 62 to 102 full-COLA Pension TDV =49429.075*40
  - » 7-year delayed pension with 40-year full-COLA TDV = $1,977,163.00

Chapter 10

How to Use This Newfound Knowledge

Practical Uses of This Knowledge

Brow furrowed from the last chapter? I don't blame you a bit. It wasn't easy writing, so it couldn't have been easy reading. I applaud your perseverance and apologize if you found my verbal skills less than adequate when explaining the formulas. That said, let's try to bring the theoretical down to the practical level with some applications for your newfound and hard-fought TDV knowledge. Specifically, I want to talk about practical ways you can use TDV in your *Golden Albatross* decision-making process. I'll also expand on some points I made in the previous chapter about using TDV when considering a lump-sum offer. While lump-sum offers don't equate exactly to the *Golden Albatross* decision-making process, the practical knowledge TDV provides when considering a lump-sum offer is too useful to ignore.

Practical Application: TDV, Retirement Budgets, and Gap Numbers

The most practical application for your newfound IDV and TDV knowledge relates to your proposed retirement expenses. In other words, proportionally, how many of your monthly or annual retirement expenses will your pension cover? All? If so, that should weigh heavily in any *Golden Albatross* scenario to leave a job before earning your pension. Half? Not bad, but how will you cover the other expenses? Part-time job? Investments? Savings? Rental income?

Let's not get ahead of ourselves. The answers to the above questions assume you know how much you'll spend in retirement. So, at this point I ask, do you? Have you built a retirement budget?

If not, that's a problem. Not an insurmountable problem, but a problem nonetheless. I say that because the absolute best way to plan for retirement is to build a retirement budget based on:

1. How much you spend now on specific categories

2. How much you've spent in the past two-to-three years on those categories

3. How much you estimate you'll spend on those categories in the future (i.e. during retirement)

Of course, that projected budget should be based on life's circumstances. If you plan to eliminate your mortgage before retirement, adjust accordingly. Still need to pay for your kids' college? Again, adjust accordingly. Don't forget that most expenses go down the longer you get into retirement. The one exception to that rule of thumb is, of course, healthcare. Hopefully, you get my point. Building a category-by-category retirement budget based on your tracked past spending habits, plus a realistic estimate of future expenses, is the most accurate way of estimating the costs you'll face in retirement.

By categories, I mean the non-discretionary fundamentals like food, housing, healthcare, transportation, and clothing—the things you need in life. But I also mean the discretionary categories like entertainment, travel, and hobbies—the things that make life and retirement fun. If you don't track your spending to that level, I strongly urge you to start. If you need help, I will provide references for tracking your money at the end of this chapter.

Once you've built this money-tracking knowledge, then you can estimate how many of your projected retirement expenses your potential future pension will cover. Ideally, it will cover everything. Realistically, that probably won't be the case—unless you're super-frugal or have a great pension. If that's you, congratulations! The rest of us, though, will have a *Gap Number*.

What's a *Gap Number*, you ask? That's the gap between your calculated expenses in retirement and the amount you expect to earn through your fixed income (i.e. pension, social security, and annuities). Mathematically, it looks something like this:

$$\text{Gap Number} = (\text{ Fixed Expenses } + \text{ Discretionary Expenses })$$
$$- (\text{ Pension Payments } + \text{ Social Security })$$
$$\textbf{OR}$$
$$G = E - F$$

In this case, E equals total expenses and F equals total fixed income.

You want your Gap Number to be as small as possible for retirement. If your *Gap Number* is small, and your future pension is the major reason why then you should weight that knowledge accordingly for any *Golden Albatross* decision you may be contemplating. On the other hand, if your future pension only covers a small percentage of your projected retirement budget, then maybe leaving that job for greener pastures is the right move.

Help! I Don't Have Time to Track My Money

Need to make a stay-or-go decision about your pensionable job sooner rather than later? If so, that *Golden Albatross* must be weighing heavily on your soul. I'm sorry to hear that because it's not a fun place to be. Well, there are other methods for estimating retirement expenses, not all of which I endorse.

The most popular method for estimating retirement expenses is to simply take 80% of your annual pre-retirement *income* and use that as your retirement spending number. This is based on something called the 80% rule in the financial planning world. For the record, I absolutely hate this method. I fail to understand how pre-retirement income correlates to what people spend in retirement. Dig into the 80% rule and you'll see that, in fact, there is no correlation. In my opinion, the only reason so many financial advisors and planners use the 80% rule is that most people (i.e. their clients) hate to track their money. Thus, to use *something* as a measure for retirement planning, they default to the 80% rule.

If you're really up against the clock to make a *Golden Albatross* decision, and truly aren't prepared, I'd recommend eating the elephant in much smaller bites. Instead of trying to estimate your entire retirement budget in one go (and possibly wildly miscalculating), simply compare your pension's monthly IDV and TDV numbers against your everyday expenses. Take a month's worth of credit card and bank statements and catalog the places you spent your money. Lump all the grocery store expenses together. Do the same with all the places you ate (or drank beer). Catalog your bills like rent, electricity, and gas. Will any of those disappear in retirement? If so, toss them out.

When done, look at how many of those expenses would be covered by your future pension's monthly IDV or TDV numbers. If you do this, it will at least give you a ball-park estimate for what your future pension might cover. It won't do much beyond that, but it's better than nothing. I also think it's far better than plucking a random percentage of your pre-retirement income from the air. If you're freaking out about the need to make a *Golden Albatross* decision soon, and you don't have a monthly budget for a reliable Gap Number comparison, then check out the end of chapter resources link. I've placed some more guidance there for you.

Practical Application: Lump Sums

OK, that's enough about *Gap Numbers* and whatnot. Let's shift gears to another practical way you can use your TDV knowledge. As previously mentioned, knowing how to calculate TDV is especially handy when examining any lump-sum offer from your pension plan. It allows you to make a dollar-for-dollar comparison in today's dollars, without the need for any funky inflation calculations. For example, if your pension has a CPI-linked COLA and your work's lump-sum offer is $200K, but you just calculated a $1 million TDV, it means the offer is 80% less than what you're owed over your expected lifetime.

Of course, your pension fund manager will argue that the reduced lump sum's value was based on the accounting principle known as the Time Value of Money (TVM). In other words, they reduced your lump sum even more than inflation's effect because they assume you'll invest the money. Thus, as they see it, they don't need to pay you as much in the present because compounding interest and/or compounding rates of return will do the work for them (and you) by growing that lump sum to an amount that's similar to your TDV.

While I don't dispute the effects of TVM, I'd be wary of this line of argument in specific connection to pension lump-sum calculations. First, it's highly likely that you won't get as good of an investment return (interest rate) on your lump sum than what the fund managers used to calculate your lump-sum offer. Why? For one, there are some legal loopholes in the way lump sums are calculated that pretty much guarantee this.

Also, retail investors (i.e. you and me) have a historically awful average rate of return on investments in comparison to the indices like the S&P 500. Financial planners and advisors don't have that much of a better record either, once you remove their fees. If you don't believe me, just Google the Dalbar Report for whatever respective year that you're interested in, and you'll find plenty of articles about how much, and why, people suck at investing.

In the meantime, by taking a lump sum you're legally letting the pension fund off the hook. You excuse them from paying you what you're owed, and what you'd otherwise get if you elected annuity payments for the future—assuming your pension fund is on solid financial ground. As we discussed in the Pension Safety Chapter though, depending on the fund, any assumption about financial stability may be a big one. It's yet another reason your pension lump sum is reduced.

By offering the lump sum, the pension fund is legally stating that they can't guarantee they'll be around in the future to payout. Thus, they'll pay you now. However, since they're doing you the favor by paying you a guaranteed amount now, versus an unguaranteed but legally calculated amount in the future, they're going to charge you for the convenience. In other words, they are taking some off the top for insurance, and like most insurance of this type, it isn't cheap.

I've discovered lump sums are a hot topic. Not only that but, if you couldn't tell, I get worked up about the less-than-fair manner that lump sums are calculated. However, while using TDV when considering a lump-sum offer is completely practical, lump sums themselves don't really play into the *Golden Albatross* decision. They're more of a potential outcome.

In other words, you may/may not be more likely to take a lump sum, depending on your *Golden Albatross* decision. Obviously, you're not going to get a lump-sum offer if you decided to leave a job before *vesting* in the pension! Thus, lump-sum analysis is a topic probably best left to a future book about what to do **after** you make your *Golden Albatross* decision. In case you're already at that point, I placed lump-sum related resources at the end of this chapter.

Practical Application Limitations

Finally, one cautionary note. TDV is strictly a cumulative sum of the monetary compensation owed to a pensioner by the pension fund through an annuity over an Estimated Life Span (ELS). As I showed you in Chapter 9, TDV can be calculated in year one retirement dollars, or present dollars. However, TDV does not include the estimated value of any Other Post-Retirement Benefits (OPRBs) like healthcare! If by leaving a pensionable job, you are also leaving OPRBs on the table, you must take the TDV techniques applicable to your pension from Chapter 9, and combine it with the Mathemagic technique I will demonstrate in Chapter 12.

As a result, don't put this book down just yet, because there is still more to learn! By combining the two methods, you can obtain a far more comprehensive estimate of the total monetary value of your pension. It's typically enough of a differential to make your *Golden Albatross* decision a lot harder.

And of course, there's the hybrid scenario where a person contemplates quitting a pensionable job in which they are *partially vested* in the pension. As stated in Chapter 8, many pension plans offer *partial vesting* after an initial number of years on the job. This is also known as *gradual vesting*. However, pension funds often restrict full pension benefits and OPRBs, like healthcare, to those who work long enough to *fully vest*.

In that specific instance, where a worker is *partially vested* (or close to it) and suffering from the existential crisis that is the *Golden Albatross*, a TDV calculation should not only be possible but also helpful. In fact, a decision to stay until the *partial vesting* point might offer someone a great compromise between leaving a job that is toxic (for whatever reason) but also with something to show "for the effort."

If nothing else, making a TDV calculation for the *partially vested* pension amount would assist the worker if/when the pension fund offers a lump sum. A lot of pension funds like to offer departing employees, who are *partially vested*, a lump sum. This allows the fund to clear that future obligation from their books at a relatively low cost. What a TDV can't do for a worker in that situation is provide the total value of a *fully vested* pension if OPRBs are in play. Again, that would require combining the techniques from Chapter 9 with techniques I will explain in Chapter 12.

Interested in more information on tracking your money, pension lump sums, and/or further discussions on the *Gap Number* concept?
Check out the Chapter 10 resources at: https://grumpusmaximus.com/golden-albatross-book-chapter-resources/chapter-10/

- Numerous practical applications exist for TDV

- Use TDV to help determine your *Gap Number*

- $G = E - F$

- Track your money, for multiple years if possible. It's the most effective method for estimating retirement expenses

- If you can't track expenses, then use monthly IDV/TDV to compare to your everyday expenses

- TDV is extremely useful when considering a lump-sum offer from a pension fund that doesn't include OPRBs

- TDV is also useful for workers departing a pension fund in which they are *partially vested*, but not *fully vested*

- TDV, in and of itself, cannot be used to determine the value of a pension with OPRBs, like healthcare, attached to full vesting. That requires a mix of TDV techniques from Chapter 9, and yet to be discussed techniques in Chapter 12

Chapter 11
Valuing Pension Subsidized Healthcare

A Sin of Omission

Confession time! When I covered how to calculate the Total Dollar Value (TDV) of your pension in Chapter 9, I purposely restricted the calculations to retirement income only. I didn't include Other Post-Retirement Benefits (OPRBs), alternately known as Other Earned Benefits (OEBs). For those of you unfamiliar with OPRBs, Investopedia defines them as:

> *Benefits, other than pension distributions, paid to employees during their retirement years. Most post-retirement benefits include life insurance and medical plans.*

Some other examples of OPRBs include tuition assistance, legal advice, and support for funeral arrangements. I excluded OPRBs from my TDV calculations primarily because they are hard to value, and don't necessarily come with price tags attached. In the U.S. at least, no better example of this exists than pension-linked or subsidized healthcare.

A Grumpus History of U.S. Healthcare

My international readers with access to universal healthcare coverage might be confused as to why some pensions in the U.S. have healthcare linked to them (and therefore they may want to skip this chapter altogether). However, it's because the closest thing to universal healthcare coverage and a national healthcare system in the U.S. starts at age 65. It's a program called Medicare. Thus, if you retire before age 65, you need to figure out a way to finance your healthcare. Depending on which state a person lives in, and on how poor they appear on their income tax returns, a person might qualify for a different type of safety net healthcare coverage called Medicaid, even if they are young.

Outside of those two government-funded systems, retirees under the age of 65 (and their working counterparts) have three options:

1. Purchase healthcare coverage on the private insurance market
2. Rely on some subsidized version of the same through their (former) employer (if offered)
3. Run the risk and go without

Each of those options is problematic in its own right, but combined they create a perfect storm for retirement planning chaos. That's especially bad if you're trying to account for healthcare costs in a realistic retirement budget before you retire.

The 2010 Affordable Care Act (ACA), or Obamacare in the vernacular, attempted to reform the U.S. healthcare system by expanding the number of people under the age of 65 (both healthy and sick) covered by either Medicaid or the private health insurance industry. It sought to do this through a combination of increased Federal subsidies to State

Medicaid systems and directly to U.S. taxpayers, forcing insurance companies to eliminate exclusion clauses for pre-existing health conditions, creating tax penalties for individuals or families who chose to go without healthcare, and creating requirements for companies over a certain size to offer their workers subsidized healthcare.

So far, the ACA has met with mixed results. It expanded healthcare coverage to approximately 20 million more people than before. It did this mostly by providing an opportunity for previously ill and currently poor people to obtain healthcare coverage. However, it didn't create a painful enough tax penalty to force healthier and younger citizens to join the private health insurance markets in enough numbers to offset the costs of that expansion.

Not only that but in 2018 the Trump administration eliminated the tax penalty within the ACA starting in tax year 2019. Thus, healthy young people have even less incentive to obtain healthcare coverage. As a result, the ACA increased health insurance costs for families who pay for their coverage versus obtaining it through an employer-sponsored program. It also increased business costs for employers that provide subsidized healthcare to their employees.

The ACA was created by a Democrat-controlled Congress and Executive Branch without support from the Republican opposition. That created a lot of political acrimony which fostered dozens of Republican-led Congressional and Judicial efforts to overturn it. As of October 2019, the ACA has survived those challenges fundamentally intact. However, the ACA's mixed bag of results, along with the political acrimony its establishment created, continues to draw calls from the current Republican-controlled Executive and Senate to "repeal and replace" it. In the meantime, the current batch of 2020 Democratic presidential candidates seems transfixed on the "Medicare for All" proposal originally championed in 2016, and regurgitated in 2019, by Senator Bernie Sanders.

Please don't interpret this overview as an endorsement of one side or the other. It's meant merely as an observation on how much has changed over the past eight years, and how much it may change in the near future based on the politics that currently swirl around the U.S. healthcare system.

A Uniquely American Impasse

It's important to note that the ACA didn't fundamentally change the U.S. healthcare system. That was never its intent. It only sought to expand the pool of covered people through a few large tweaks to the previous system. Even before the ACA, the U.S. healthcare system was already the most expensive in the world in terms of cost to taxpayers. It was also nowhere near as comprehensive in its coverage or as effective in its delivery as the 13 most developed countries in the world. Unfortunately, the ACA has done little to make the system more efficient.

What does all this mean? Well, for many Americans, healthcare is either a system that goes too far towards socialized medicine or doesn't go far enough. It is a point of view that correlates strongly to a person's political affiliation.

Regardless of their political stripes, though, I would hope all Americans can at least agree the U.S. ended up with an idiosyncratic and inefficient bastardization of both free-market and socialized healthcare systems that serves few of its citizens particularly efficiently. Instead of cherry-picking the best ideas from both ends of the political spectrum, or at least striving for the mediocrity that pragmatic political compromise often produces, the U.S. seemingly muddled its way into an overpriced, substandard healthcare quagmire.

The Golden Albatross vs. Healthcare Costs

Why does any of this matter to someone writing a Financial Independence (FI) book dedicated to those who earn pensions? There are two reasons. The first is that the healthcare system as described above, which relies heavily on employer-subsidized healthcare, potentially holds many readers hostage during their *Golden Albatross* moment. They may find themselves in an insufferable job situation, but choose to stay purely for healthcare coverage. I don't think that's a particularly fair system on a personal level. Nor do I believe it to be a particularly efficient economic system at the national level in terms of human capital and the free flow of labor.

Now, I might be willing to accept the first issue, if it were not for this second issue. That's the fact that the U.S. healthcare system, and all the uncertainty surrounding it, makes it impossible to realistically plan for retirement healthcare costs before the age of 65 (Medicare). That's especially true *IF* a person (or family) doesn't have access to one of the subsidized healthcare options I described above. By that I mean private healthcare costs are fluctuating so much on an annual basis within the insurance markets that a person cannot effectively estimate how much they need to save for the next year, let alone invest to pay for their health insurance in far off future years. In other words, it's a total crapshoot.

Given the fact that you've made it this far into the book, you know how much I emphasize planning for retirement. Chris Mamula gets to the crux of the retirement planning problem that healthcare poses over at the Can I Retire Yet? blog:

> *Consider this example given in an analysis by the Kaiser Family Foundation if ACA subsidies go away. They note, "...a low-income 60-year-old could get a silver plan for $83 per month (with ACA*

subsidies) but would have to pay $775 per month if he bought that plan without a subsidy, plus he would have a higher deductible because he would no longer benefit from cost-sharing subsidies that are only available on the exchange." Using the "Rule of 300", and plugging in the ranges from the example above means that projected savings needed for health insurance premiums would range from $24,900 ($83×300) to $232,500 ($775×300).

Holy schnikes! Did I quote that passage correctly? I just checked, and indeed, I quoted that passage correctly. That's almost ten times more from the bottom to the top of that cost scale! How does anyone plan for such a wide variety of costs in their retirement plan? They don't.

As Chris points out in his post, he and his wife couldn't plan for something so nebulous. One of them had to keep working at least part-time to obtain healthcare through an employer. Currently, that responsibility falls to his wife, since she loves her part-time job. I think it stinks that a couple who would otherwise be able to plan and save enough money for health insurance in early retirement cannot do so simply because it's impossible to effectively estimate potential future healthcare costs. However, their less than ideal situation also proves my first point about how this system can hold people hostage. This should matter to all readers of a personal finance book.

Not to leave you hanging, Chris and his wife built some other options so his wife doesn't feel trapped.

Grumpus's Point

OK, up to this point I've ranted about how much the U.S. healthcare system sucks, and how hard the current conditions make planning for the future. But how does it relate to the topic of this book? Well, the entire point of this book is to provide a method and means for dissecting the multitude of issues surrounding the idea of the *Golden Albatross*. I'm doing this to help you determine if it's *worth it* to stick it out and earn your pension.

As I've pointed out in Chapter 8, all pensions are not created equal, which means some pensions are objectively more *worth it* than others. However, that doesn't take into consideration your circumstances. The best I can do is to help you identify how valuable your potential pension is. Or I can try because in the case of pension subsidized healthcare, that's a tall order.

By painting that depressingly realistic picture of the state of U.S. healthcare above, it should be obvious just how important a pension that provides some form of stable subsidized healthcare can be. That's especially true for anyone looking to retire before age 65. I might go so far as to label it *invaluable*. This would contrast significantly with other parts of this book where I demonstrate how valuable specific aspects of a pension can be.

In the case of pension subsidized healthcare though, I can't help you place a dollar value on it with any kind of accuracy. That's due to the range of magnitude in the cost window that Chris Mamula described in his article. Does anyone have a crystal ball that can determine the future of the U.S. healthcare system? No? Well, until then, pension subsidized healthcare will remain a wildcard when determining your pension's value.

Final Thoughts on Healthcare and Pensions

That said, I weight any pension with subsidized healthcare heavily towards the *highly valuable* end of the scale. In Chapter 8, I identified the following common features that make some pensions more valuable than others. The most valuable pensions:

- Vest workers after short periods of employment
- Use high-income averages and percentage multipliers in their IDV formulas
- Start payouts immediately upon retirement
- Provide Consumer Price Index-linked Cost of Living Allowance (COLA) for the entire pension amount

It's time to amend that list (for my U.S. readers at least), and include a pension with subsidized healthcare coverage as one of its OPRBs. How high on the importance list do I place subsidized healthcare coverage? I'd say that depends on your circumstances. If you're retiring close to 65, then it's probably not as important because Medicare is about to kick in. On the other hand, if you're retiring at 45, I'd say it's second only in importance to a pension that starts to payout immediately.

Interestingly enough, I've interacted with some folks in the FI space who say pension subsidized healthcare is the singular most important feature of their pension. That may be an appropriate assessment if they have a lot of medical issues. If healthcare costs continue to inflate faster than the rest of the CPI, maybe we all should rate it that high. That's the frustrating point of this entire chapter. Without some certainty on where the U.S. healthcare system is heading and the costs associated with it, an objective determination about the value of your pension subsidized healthcare is extremely hard to make. Unfortunately, it's purely subjective, even though it shouldn't be.

I can relate 100% to anyone stuck in a *Golden Albatross* moment who's uncertain about what they should do based on healthcare. I was there a few years ago. Ultimately, I decided to stay and earn that pension. I based part of that decision on the heavily subsidized healthcare coverage the military will provide me for the rest of my life, as well as my spouse.

For anyone who's decided to stick it out for a pension in which the healthcare coverage starts immediately upon retirement, you have a powerful tool at your disposal to shape your retirement in ways many others do not. This especially holds for those, like me, who aim to retire in their mid-40s or early 50s. I would encourage you to safeguard that tool and use it wisely.

—

Interested in some potential resources that may help you determine the value of your work/pension subsidized healthcare?
Check out the Chapter 11 resources at: https://grumpusmaximus.com/golden-albatross-book-chapter-resources/chapter-11/

END OF CHAPTER TAKEAWAYS

- The U.S. healthcare system is a mess. So much so, that it makes objective planning for retirement healthcare costs difficult, if not impossible
- Recent estimates on the future price of healthcare coverage in the U.S. range on a scale of up to 10 times more expensive from top to bottom
- In a country like the U.S. that doesn't provide universal healthcare coverage before age 65, a pension with subsidized healthcare coverage linked to it is valuable
- In those situations, Grumpus Maximus recommends you add it as a fifth point to the list of "what makes one pension more valuable than others"
- This issue impacts a *Golden Albatross* decision, too. Work subsidized healthcare is an extremely powerful incentive to stay in a job, even if staying isn't in the overall best interest of the worker
- Anyone who's decided to stay and earn a pension with subsidized healthcare, especially if it starts immediately upon retirement, has access to an early retirement planning tool that most others don't
- Use it wisely

THE GOLDEN ALBATROSS

PART THREE

Chapter 12
The Grumpmatic and Mathemagic Comparison Methods

One Plus Two Equals Three

Finally! We made it to Part 3 of the book. I feel like throwing a parade for just getting this far. Let's be honest, unless you love numbers and making calculations, Part 2 was kind of dry. It was *worth it*, though, because you'll soon find out that Part 3 ties everything from Parts 1 and 2 together. This is where the subjective and objective meet to help you make that *worth vs. worth it* decision. At least that's the intent. And, since the whole of Part 3 is really a review of Parts 1 and 2, I don't need to review what I just wrote! This means we can get right to it!

Choose Your Own Adventure

We've come to the part of the book where I show you how to take the subjective issues discussed in Part 1 of the book, and compare them to the (mostly) objective numbers calculated in Part 2. Don't fool yourself, this won't be clean. On the other hand, it isn't necessarily hard work. Or maybe, more appropriately put, it's as hard as you choose to make it—which is why I've provided two different methods for you to choose from.

I provide one method for the feelers out there, who'd rather not get into the job of numerically weighting the importance of their subjective feelings about their job. The other method is for the objective number crunchers, who want to quantify everything. I'd actually encourage you to run through both methods. Doing so will ensure that your feelings and numbers are aligned with your ultimate decision. However, I can't force you to do that, so really, it's up to you to use or dispense with these methods as you see fit.

The Grumpmatic Method

Although I doubt anyone will ever confuse it with the Socratic Method, the Grumpmatic Method is my thought experiment for making a relatively logical *Golden Albatross* decision while still allowing for emotional considerations. I liken it to building a scale in your mind that balances an objective valuation of your pension on one side against the desires, wants, needs, or fears motivating you to leave a pensionable job on the other. I developed this method for the less mathematically inclined who need to feel their way through decisions as much as they need to think through them.

I don't mean that as an insult. Some people are *thinkers* and some are *feelers*. The world needs both. Therefore, the Grumpmatic Method should feel intuitive for anyone who's read the entire book up to this point, because I've addressed many of the issues on both sides of the scales already.

Let's discuss the objective side of the scale first. For the objective side of the scale, I recommend utilizing my list of the most valuable pension features identified in Chapters 8 and 11. The inclusion of these five features in a pension makes it objectively more valuable than those without. Those features are:

1. Short vestment periods

2. Initial Dollar Value (IDV) calculated using formulas with high-income averages and percentage multipliers

3. Payments that start immediately upon retirement

4. Entire pension amounts that adjust annually using a Consumer Price Index-linked Cost of Living Allowance (COLA)

5. Pension subsidized healthcare (in the U.S. at least)

If you're lucky enough to have a pension with all five features, then congratulations are in order because you have the Cadillac or Mercedes Benz of pensions. You can objectively weight your pension as *more valuable* on the Grumpmatic scale. Conversely, the fewer of these features in your pension, the less valuable it is. Thus, the less you should weight your pension on the objective side of the Grumpmatic scale.

Personally, I'd say if your pension possesses three of the five features, you have a *valuable* pension. Alternatively, if your pension has one or none of the features, your pension is *less valuable*. Play around with those labels as you see fit. They're not set in stone. In fact, depending on your personal circumstances, some of the features may be more valuable to you than others. For instance, pension subsidized healthcare is a feature that many people place high on the *valuable* list, to the point where it may outweigh all other considerations.

Another objective criterion you may want to consider is how big or small your future pension would make your *Gap Number*. Remember, your *Gap Number* is the amount of your projected retirement (or post-work) expenses that your fixed income, like a pension annuity, won't cover. So, if you've done your money tracking homework like I discussed in Chapter 10, and your *Gap Number* is small because your future pension will cover most or all of your projected retirement expenses, then it's objectively more valuable than a pension that doesn't.

I would also add the reminder here that the money your pension represents isn't the end, but rather the means to achieve a goal. Maybe that goal is to spend more time with your grandkids while not worrying about your financial stability, or maybe it's to travel around the world on a slow vacation. Either way, if by looking at your post-work budget you can objectively say that a pending pension would unlock or enable some sort of lifelong dream or goal, then definitely, weight it accordingly. The inverse is also true. If the pension won't move the needle on unlocking your retirement dreams, don't weight it.

Speaking of weighting considerations, which motivating desires, wants, needs, or fears should you place as a counterbalance on the other side of the Grumpmatic scales? I recommend starting with fear for your pension's safety. Emphasizing fear for your pension's safety on the subjective side is weird since I placed assessing your pension's likelihood of safety in the supposedly objective part of the book. However, by determining if your pension is safe or not, you determine if your fears are founded...or not. As explained in Chapter 7, understanding the likelihood of your pension fund failing to meet its future financial obligations is a key to determining whether or not staying at your pensionable job is *worth it*. It may be the most important, actually.

What else could go on the counter-balance side of the Grumpmatic scales? Considering how much I talked about it, I think inflation is another worthy issue to consider. Specifically, if your pension does not have some sort of inflation-linked COLA, it's worth considering your fear level with regards to inflation. Remember the Star Wars conversation from Chapter 8 where I discussed inflation's nefarious effects on your pension? Certainly, a rampant inflation scenario like the U.S. faced in the 1970s would quickly destroy the value of any non-inflation-linked COLA pension.

Yet, how likely is that? As pointed out in Chapter 8, the average inflation rate stands at 3.22%, and on a macro scale has fallen steadily in the U.S. for decades. Furthermore, since 2007 the U.S. inflation rate has averaged only 2%. That said, as I demonstrated in Chapter 8 and 9, even a 2% inflation rate can eat away at a pension's value over time. So, if you're looking at a lengthy retirement timeline and your pension doesn't have a COLA, then definitely address your concern over inflation on this side of the scale.

What else? Certainly, personal health considerations and family impacts like I discussed in Chapters 1 and 6 deserve consideration on the subjective side. I believe it's important to note that you need not face health issues as serious as my friend's from Chapter 1, or mine from Chapter 6. Our cases are extreme examples in comparison to the health impacts of most pensionable jobs. On the other hand, if you find yourself in unfortunate circumstances connected to your pensionable job and your personal health, then weigh those issues accordingly. Don't ignore them and concentrate solely on the money side of the equation. That's a sure recipe for disaster.

In any case, as I stated in Chapter 5, everyone needs to determine for themselves when "enough is enough." What's acceptable for one person won't be for another. It all comes down to how much of your precious life force and health you're willing to sacrifice to achieve the financial stability that your potential pension represents.

There's no correct answer to that question, by the way. Personal finance and health issues are just that, personal. So, again, please don't compare your situation to mine or my friend's. If anything, remember that in hindsight I believe I made the wrong decision. As a result, I was stuck making lemonade out of a shit sandwich. Don't let that be you!

Hopefully, by now you get the point of the Grumpmatic Method. There are any number of items you could consider as a counter-balance to the objectively valuable features. Remember, though, some are more legitimate than others. Personal health, pension safety, and inflation... legitimate. The fact that you hate your job...not so legitimate. As discussed in Chapter 5, drill down to the core problem. Don't simply accept the main symptom of your job dissatisfaction as the root cause.

Ultimately, once you figure out the criteria on both sides of the scale, you will need to determine which side outweighs the other. There's no objectively correct answer since this process is intuitive and based on your personal circumstances. The process is merely a thought exercise, but one with some rigor since it utilizes your newfound pension knowledge.

I recommend you write everything down and look at the two sides of the scale on paper. Not only will you have a written record of why you made your decision, but it should also help crystalize your thought process. Remember, there's power in the written word so pay attention to which side of the scale speaks most to you once you write everything down. If, for some reason, that sounds like too much work, then just wait until Chapter 13. I will reward your procrastination with a visual aid that does a lot of the work for you. Ideally, it should make feeling your way to a *Golden Albatross* decision a lot easier.

Grumpus Maximus in Mathemagic Land

Anyone remember the Disney® cartoon from which I riffed the above section title? My 7th-grade math teacher showed it to us because he thought the scene where Donald Duck shoots pool using geometry lessons was cool. Unfortunately, I'm not about to take you on a *groovy* adventure to a world of mathematics, wonder, and shooting pool. No, I chose the section title because the calculations we're about to make really are more Mathemagic than mathematics. In other words, don't let the following equations fool you and don't fall in love with the numbers. They are more art than science. I suggest you use them as a guide.

With that said, I didn't simply make these equations up. As I demonstrated in Chapter 9, calculating the Total Dollar Value (TDV) of your pension in today's dollars is possible. In fact, I believe you can get a fairly accurate understanding of exactly how valuable your pension is by doing so.

However, the TDV calculations require you to estimate your lifespan, and possibly the future inflation rate, depending on the features of your pension. Since TDV is used in some of the follow-on equations below, which include other estimates, a level of uncertainty builds into the final value fairly quickly. This is why I refer to the outcome as a ROM (Rough Order of Magnitude) value, rather than the absolute value of the money you might lose by leaving a pensionable career. Enough with the caveats though; let's get to the calculations.

In **Step 1**: you cut a hole in the box! Just kidding.

Instead, you estimate your Total Pension Value (TPV) by adding the TDV (determined in Chapter 9) to the estimated value of any Other Post-Retirement Benefits (OPRBs) like healthcare (as discussed in Chapter 11):

$$\text{Total Pension Value (TPV)} =$$
$$\text{Total Dollar Value (TDV)} + \text{Value of any OPRBs}$$

Right about now is where you remind me that I copped out in Chapter 11 because I couldn't determine a method for calculating the value of pension subsidized healthcare. True, but as I just pointed out, we are calculating a Rough Order of Magnitude (ROM) here. So, if your pension carries subsidized healthcare as an OPRB, then you need to value it. Whether that's on the lower or higher end of the $25,000 to $232,000 scale that Chris Mamula calculated, or some number you determine yourself (see the end of chapter resources for Chapter 11), you still need a number.

Given the uncertainty over healthcare in the U.S., I'd advise caution and tell any U.S. based person to pick a higher value for pension subsidized healthcare, rather than a lower number. Take or leave that advice as you see fit because I'm no healthcare expert. Whatever number you come up with for healthcare, don't forget your pension may have other benefits attached to it like life insurance. If so, add that value in as well.

For **Step 2**, take your TPV and divide it by the Expected Life Span (ELS) that you used in your TDV calculation in Chapter 9. It's important to use the same ELS number from your TDV calculation. Otherwise, you inject even more inaccuracy into your ROM. For the purposes of this book, I used 40 years as the ELS in the examples in Chapter 9, so that's what I'll use in the examples below. In any case, once you determine ELS, use it to divide your TPV. When done, you end up with your Annual Pension Value (APV).

$$APV = TPV / ELS$$

Step 3 requires a little bit of research into Safe Withdrawal Rates (SWRs) before making your calculation. Specifically, you need to determine which SWR you intend to use for your calculation. The original 4% SWR is still the standard that most financial planners use in their calculations. However, newer research shows that the rate may be either too conservative or too aggressive, depending on your personal situation.

Since I don't know your personal situation, I can only tell you mine. Worst case scenario, assuming my wife and I never work again, I'm looking at a 40+ year retirement when I'm finished with the military. Thus, I tend to go conservative and use the 3.5% Rule of Thumb proposed by Big ERN (aka Karsten) who writes the blog Early Retirement Now.

You might want to use a different SWR rate, and that's OK. However, if you are planning a retirement that's longer than 30 years, or if you are an international (non-U.S.) reader/investor, I would counsel the same amount of caution as respected retirement researcher Wade Pfau. As he noted in a recent interview, Bill Bengen's original 4% SWR was built around a 30-year retirement model and domestic U.S. investments. Change either of those inputs and a 4% SWR doesn't work nearly as well. So, given those points, and the fact that my example from Chapter 9 uses 40-year ELS, I'm going to use a 3.5% SWR in my examples below.

Once you decide on your SWR, change it to a decimal. For me, that means a 3.5% SWR changes to .035. If you used a 4% SWR, then it would turn into .04. Whatever the case, use that decimal version of your SWR to divide your APV. I call that value the Equivalent Invested Value (EIV). Thus, the formula to determine your EIV looks like this:

$$EIV = APV / SWR$$

The EIV is your *money* number—literally and figuratively. This number literally tells you how much money you would need to save and invest upon retirement to replicate your pension's potential income stream, and all of its OPRBs, by utilizing an SWR. It's the investment nest egg equivalent to your pension with all of its perks. Or, in other words, it's a self-built pension.

Figuratively, this value can help you determine whether or not leaving a pensionable job, for a non-pensionable job, would be *worth it*. You can do this by judging whether or not the non-pensionable job would pay enough to amass your pension's EIV by the time you retire. If the job is high paying enough and/or the promotion opportunities good enough, then the probabilities might be high that you could amass the EIV before retirement. The opposite is also true. Obviously, it would all depend on just how high of an EIV you get when you run the numbers.

Finally, I draw your attention to something I briefly touched on in Chapter 10. EIV provides a great contrast for those considering a departure from a pensionable job in which they are *partially vested*. This assumes OPRBs, like healthcare, are attached to *full vesting*. If so, your *fully vested* pension's EIV would be radically higher than the TDV for the *partially vested* pension you calculated based on the formulas in Chapter 9.

If you don't believe me, just run the below EIV example without the healthcare valuation, and see what you get. Then compare the no-healthcare EIV to the EIV with healthcare. You'll see there's a 25% difference, and that's with all other considerations being equal. Just imagine what the EIV would be for a reduced TDV based on a *partially vested* pension. It would be a *helluva* lot less. And yes, that's a technical military term which stretches all the way back to World War II.

Mathemagic Example

OK, let's run one example to see how this EIV stuff works. You may or may not recall in Chapter 9 I calculated my pension's TDV as $2,271,138 over a 40-year ELS in retirement year one dollars. As I pointed out in Chapter 11 though, my pension also comes with subsidized healthcare as the main OPRB. For the sake of this example, let's say I estimated the healthcare coverage has a value of $750K over my lifetime. Thus, my TPV would be $3,021,138.

STEP 1

$2,271,138 (TDV) + $750K (OPRB) = $3,021,138 (TPV)

Next, I want to calculate APV. To do so I take that $3,021,138 TPV and divide it by my 40-year ELS.

STEP 2

$3,021,138 (TPV) / 40 years (ELS) = $75,528 (APV)

Finally, I determine my EIV by dividing my $75,528 APV by a decimalized version of my 3.5% SWR.

STEP 3

$75,528 (APV) / .035 (SWR) = $2,157,955 (EIV)

To make this example more poignant, put yourself in my position a few years ago. I had just suffered a mental breakdown. It occurred roughly three years before my twenty-year mark in the U.S. military, and I was unsure whether or not I could make it through the final three years to earn my pension. At the same time, I had no idea how much money I'd leave on the table if I chose to walk away. Remember, the U.S. military pension system was then and still is an all or nothing, cliff vesting, system. Either a service member makes it to twenty years and earns a pension with OPRBs, or they don't. Thus, I needed a method to calculate the potential cost of walking away.

The above method is similar to what I came up with. When I calculated my numbers, I came up with an EIV close to the $2,157,955. However, when I looked at my investment portfolio, it was nowhere near $2,157,955 in value. Furthermore, the likelihood of finding a job in the civilian sector that would pay me enough to cover that difference in three short years was close to zero. So, I had my answer. I would stay and gut it out. Doing anything else would've been something akin to financial suicide. As a result, I doubled down on my work with my mental health professionals.

What about Pension Safety in Mathemagic Land?

Great question! Finally, in Step 4 you can choose to adjust your EIV to account for the likelihood of the pension fund defaulting or declaring bankruptcy. Maybe you want to get super nerdy and use something like Bayes' Theorem to model the probability of this happening. If there is enough data available, it would certainly buy down some uncertainty within your final ROM. Or maybe you just want to look and see how far under 100% your pension is funded, and shave that amount off of your EIV. Whichever method you use to come up with a number, express it as the decimal equivalent of a percentage (0.0

through 1.00). Plug it into the right-hand portion of the equation below, run the calculations, and you should get a ROM for what I call the Adjusted Estimated Investment Amount (AEIV).

$$\text{Adjusted EIV (AEIV)} =$$
$$\text{EIV} - [\text{EIV} \times (\text{\% likelihood of DBP fund failure})]$$

As an example, let's say you're reading your pension fund's latest annual report, and it states that the funding level is 80%. You decide that means there's a 20% likelihood that the pension fund fails, and doesn't payout. As a result, you want to adjust the EIV from my above example down by 20% to adjust for the likelihood the pension fund fails. To do that, it looks like this:

$$\$2{,}157{,}955\ (\text{EIV}) - [\ \$2{,}157{,}955\ (\text{EIV}) \times .20\ ] =$$
$$\$1{,}726{,}363\ (\text{AEIV})$$

As you see from the Step 4 calculation, the higher the estimate of trouble for the pension fund, the larger the discount or adjustment, to the EIV. Of course, if you work in the U.S. and have a private or a union-administered pension, AEIV completely ignores the potential for the Pension Benefit Guaranty Corporation (PBGC) to step in and continue making some sort of pension payments.

However, as I point out in Chapter 7, despite the PBGC being a U.S. government-backed insurance agency whose sole purpose is to insure private and union pension funds against failure, parts of the PBGC are severely underfunded—specifically, the Multi-Employer Pension (MEP) fund. Thus, if the PBGC steps in to bail out a MEP pension fund, you should expect a major reduction in your payments. I will leave it to your discretion to determine how to effectively represent that in the equations above.

Clear as Mud?

I cringe at the thought of people making such an important and irreversible decision as leaving a pensionable job without due consideration. From my point of view, when someone decides to leave, they are probably leaving money on the table. Ultimately, that's OK as long as it's a deliberate and well thought out decision.

Take or leave the methods I describe above. I provided them for consideration in case you lacked a method for thinking about the problem. Depending on your preferred method for solving complex, interrelated, and emotional topics, one method might appeal more than another. My preference would be to run the Mathemagic numbers. Mrs. Grumpus would prefer the Grumpmatic Method. However, neither of us will find ourselves in that position because (for better or worse) I stayed for my pension. If you're thinking about leaving, I don't envy you, but I sincerely hope you make a well-considered decision.

Interested in more resources that may help you create your own pension?
Check out the Chapter 12 resources at: https://grumpusmaximus.com/golden-albatross-book-chapter-resources/chapter-12/

Chapter 13

A Golden Albatross Decision Aid

Self-Evident Truths

If you're a visual learner then this short chapter is for you. You've reached the point in the book where I attempt to translate all of the previously discussed topics into a concise visual tool for use when contemplating your *Golden Albatross* decision. I chose a visual format because it provides the flexibility needed to address a wide range of scenarios for those at their *Golden Albatross* moment.

I formed this approach a few years ago while I was trying to write a money manifesto for my blog. At the time, I wanted to eliminate some ambiguity in my posts about actions I considered mandatory vs. optional when making the *Golden Albatross* decision. I also wanted to capture the steps I considered mandatory for using a pension to achieve Financial Independence (FI). However, the idea of a manifesto didn't survive first-contact with me or my readers because no one could agree on the topics.

The effort was valuable nonetheless. I realized a manifesto would create sharp dividing lines among my readership through a series of *thou shalts*. Since I wasn't looking to divide my audience, I started to look for another tool. That said, I firmly believed then, and still do now, that some actions are absolutely mandatory to achieve FI (regardless of whether or not you stand to earn a pension). Much like the Declaration of Independence, though, those truths are self-evident and don't require preaching from a soapbox. Top among those would be to:

 Track your money

 Don't spend more than you earn

 Save a significant amount of what you earn

 Eliminate or avoid (consumer) debt

 Proactively educate yourself on personal finance

 Deliberately plan for your financial future

 Invest

However, once a person gets beyond the above self-evident truths, they quickly get into the realm of what makes sense for some, but may not necessarily work for others. This led to the creation of two different decision trees:

1. The *Golden Albatross* Decision Tree

2. The Path to FI Using a Pension Decision Tree

For the purposes of this book, I chose a different type of visual aid—a table list. A table list is a little less eye-watering than a decision tree. It also allows me to list in greater detail the questions I believe a person should answer when making that tough *Golden Albatross* decision. If nothing else, consider my table list a good starting point that's easily modifiable to fit your specific situation. Since everyone's pension is a little bit different, it's logical that some folks may need to modify it. But, enough talking. Let's get to the table list!

The Grumpmatic Scales Table List

GRUMPMATIC SCALES
Is staying for your pension *worth it*?

REMAIN SIDE		LEAVE SIDE	
WHAT IS THE PENSION WORTH?	WHAT CAN THE PENSION DO FOR YOU?	HOW SAFE IS THE PENSION?	OTHER GOOD REASONS?

Total Dollar Value (TDV)?
■ Initial Dollar Value
  – High income average?
  – High percentage multiplier?
■ Vesting timelines?
■ Immediacy?
  – Delayed payout?
■ COLA?
 	
Other Post-Retired Benefits (OPRBs)?
■ Healthcare?
	Retirement objectives, goals and dreams?
	
	Projected retirement budget to meet those goals?
	■ What is your Gap Number?
	
	How much money would you need to invest to replce the pension?
	■ What is the Estimated Invested Value (EIV) of the pension?
	
	What is the Adjusted EIV (AEIV) of the pension?
		Public pension?
		■ Federal?
		■ "CRR's Public Plan Database
		  – State?
		  – Local?
		Private Pension?
		■ S&P 500 Indices report status?
		■ PBGC status?
		  – Multi-Employer Plan (MEP)?
		  – Single Employer Plan (SEP)?
			Health?
			■ Short and long-term impacts?
			■ You and your family?
			
			Family?
			■ Immediate and extended (e.g. Parents)?
			
			Better opportunities? Higher pay? Self-employed?
			■ Can you hit AEIV of pension?
			
			Already FI?
			■ Investment portfolio?
			  – What's your SWR without the pension?
			
			Coping mechanisms not working?

Slide the center of the scale L/R as needed based on answers

Better Than Brexit!

As you probably noticed while reading through my example, I specifically built it to demonstrate my Grumpmatic Method for solving the *Golden*

Albatross conundrum. And, since I addressed every subject on that example somewhere in this book, you may not need to modify the example all that much. That might be especially true if you're one of those people I referred to in Chapter 12, who thinks sketching out your own Grumpmatic scale sounds too much like hard work. If that's you, then congratufreakinlations, your procrastination just paid off because I did your homework for you! Please note I take all types of beer based products as a form of repayment for my services.

Back to the table list: when reading through it I hope you also noticed that I broke out the columns into two clear sides, Leave and Remain (which eerily mimics the two sides of the Brexit vote). Don't let the initial set-up of the table list fool you, though. Once you dig into the details of your pension, and fully examine your reasons for wanting to leave your pensionable job, you may find that the division between Leave and Remain isn't quite so clear cut (also eerily like Brexit). That's why I added the sliding triangle at the bottom. Depending on the answers in the columns above, you may need to slide that triangle left or right.

Think of the sliding triangle as the fulcrum upon which the details and facts in the above columns tip towards Remain or Leave. As a result, the answers to the bulleted questions help you determine where to place the fulcrum. For example, if the answers in the "Pension Safety" column lead you to determine that your pension fund is well-run and fully funded, then slide that triangle to the right, leaving only the "Other Good Reasons" column to tip the scales in favor of Leave.

Conversely, what if it turns out that your projected pension will be too small to help in retirement? You would slide the triangle towards the left, placing the "What Can Your Pension Do For You?" column firmly in the Leave camp. Alternatively, you may need to split a column in two in order to place some answers on the Remain side and others on the Leave side. Literally, the combinations are endless and based far more on your individual circumstances than what the above example implies.

Ideally though, the side with more columns, and/or more compelling arguments in their columns, wins. However, as I mentioned several times previously, there might be subjects like healthcare coverage or pension safety that you weigh so heavily, they trump all other factors and tip the scales in their favor. That's okay too, as long as you worked through the thought exercise, and can now clearly state your reasons for leaving or remaining. Which means unlike the Brexit vote, my table list is actually designed to deliver an outcome you can live with.

Refund Policy

Finally, what happens if the the Grumpmatic Method in table list format doesn't appeal to you? Well, as my mother-in-law told me after I asked permission to marry my wife, "No return upon sale." That said, don't throw the baby out with the bath water. Scrap the format, but keep the questions. Retool them into some way that's more useful. You're not going to hurt my feelings if you don't use my method. As stated in the preface to this book, my only goal is to show you how to inject rigor into your decision to stay at, or leave, a pensionable job. What form or format you use to apply that rigor matters not to me.

To that end, the questions within my table list are not exhaustive, but they are a good start. They represent the wide variety of issues that come into play when making a decision of such magnitude. Answering all of them will probably get you about 80% to 90% of the way towards the data you need for making your *Golden Albatross* decision. Since every pension system is unique though, no single example is going to cover every topic worthy of consideration. So, again, take the format, tweak it, heavily modify it, or scrap it all together. The point of this chapter isn't to compel everyone to use a table list or the Grumpmatic Method, but to show you a visual way to holistically look at the problem by applying the lessons in this book. Good luck!

Interested in more visual resources that may help you with personal finance decisions? Check out the Chapter 13 resources at: https://grumpusmaximus.com/golden-albatross-book-chapter-resources/ chapter-13/

Chapter 14

Putting It All Together, The Golden Albatross Financial Philosophy

The Request

In spring 2018, a military member from a mid-career service school approached me with a request. He was an instructor, so let's call him Professor X. One of Professor X's topics was personal finance as it relates to the effective management of one's career. He'd read my blog and believed several of my articles were appropriate material for his students. Thus, he asked me to speak via video-conference to his class. After we exchanged a few emails on proposed topics, legal conflicts of interest, and technical hurdles, I agreed. Before that video link though, I thought it prudent to script my remarks, and so I did.

The need to script my remarks forced me to distill numerous blog posts into one coherent speech about the *Golden Albatross* decision process. It also prompted me to develop a coherent, yet concise, Grumpus Maximus financial philosophy. As a result, I believe both the topics and the remarks through which I delivered them, make a great final chapter subject material for this book. While this chapter doesn't cover any new territory, it synthesizes almost all of the previous chapters in one place. Consider this chapter the book-end to Chapter 1.

Terms and Conditions Apply

Before we get to my scripted remarks, let's discuss the left and right boundaries Professor X and I set for that engagement. Like I said above, it took a few emails to narrow down the topics. Professor X's initial thoughts included this quote (sanitized to protect the innocent, of course):

> "In terms of what to discuss, I know I sound like I'm blowing smoke, but I truly believe that you could present on any of your topics, and the class would get something very important out of it... The things you discuss in your blog are all relevant to our students who will be facing the "10 years till retirement decision" once they finish this [course]."

My gut reaction was to tell Professor X to blow as much smoke as he wanted. Not only does it inflate my fragile ego, but it also feels good! In reality, though, I asked him for some specifics, and below is what I got in return:

> "I would recommend starting with explaining the Golden Albatross FI decision tree (with an explanation of the importance of a "Gap Number"). It creates a really good foundation for people to put their decision points in perspective. By extension, it might be helpful to cover TDV [Total Dollar Value] of the pension and healthcare; compared to jettisoning from this family-unfriendly lifestyle...and what the opportunity cost would be (yes, I realize I just rolled up about four separate blog posts into one long run-on sentence, but they all seem to be the critical components of the math to make an educated decision)."

Professor X's request looked reasonable to me, so I wrote him back and told him so. Consequently, I delivered the majority of the prepared comments below for Professor X's class in 2018.

The following year, Professor X's replacement (let's call her Professor Y), contacted me. She was a student in Professor X's 2018 class, and one of the students I originally addressed. She liked the speech so much, that she asked me to deliver it to her students. Her only request was an update covering the changes in my life during the intervening time between 2018 and 2019. I added those 2019 paragraphs under the *2019 Epilogue* section at the end of this chapter. My 2018 and 2019 scripted remarks compose the remainder of this chapter.

Stick to the Script

Good afternoon everyone. It's my understanding that after the Active Duty Service Obligation (ADSO) you incur through attendance at this course, many of you will reach the ten-year mark in your career. As with numerous active duty career fields, the ten-year mark represents a major decision point—not only from a professional but also from a financial standpoint. Thus, I hope certain parts of my story resonate enough to assist each of you when you hit that career milestone.

You may be wondering why I am speaking today on this topic? The answer is in my story. I'll warn you upfront: you may find parts of what I'm about to say upsetting. I've purposely chosen not to gloss over troublesome events because I want this story to stick. So much so, that each of you walks away determined to plan better, or at least set yourself up for better choices than I did.

Hit 'em Hard

I sit before you almost two years (to the day) after I suffered a mental breakdown. In the spring of 2016, I was diagnosed with mixed depressive-anxiety disorder due to Post-Traumatic Stress (PTS). The primary cause of my PTS was a decision I made in December 2012 to deploy to Afghanistan...a week after my wife miscarried our second pregnancy. As events unfolded, I was afforded the choice to skip the deployment. At the time, though, I believed I owed it to the person I was relieving (in Afghanistan) to deploy. I also felt compelled to go for the good of my career and the long-term financial stability of my family. Without the deployment, my next promotion was questionable. Failing to promote would have subjected me to the risk of a Continuation Board.

To put this story in full context, my breakdown didn't go without warning signs or some sort of buildup. By October 2009 I was susceptible to future traumatic events because I was almost killed on a deployed mission. I chose to ignore the now obvious side effects that resulted from that close call. Looking further back in my career, that susceptibility may have begun as early as mid-2003 when a co-worker, friend, and mentor of mine was killed in the nascent stages of the insurgency in Iraq. Not only did I choose to ignore the potential impact of these events on my mental health, but I failed to heed the personal doubts that started to develop about my calling and chosen profession.

It's important to note that at this point in my career (December 2012) I hadn't educated myself financially. As a result, I didn't understand my alternative financial or career choices. Strangely, my family's financial situation at the time was healthy enough to absorb the impact of those alternative choices; I was simply ignorant of the options. In hindsight that elective ignorance appears costly. It took a few years for the PTS to finally manifest, but manifest it did. By spring 2016, my deployment decision had cost me a good bit of my health and happiness.

The Financial Problem

Ironically, I've always been a good saver. Once married, despite a few hiccups, my wife and I both continued good saving behavior. However, there's a difference between simply saving, and saving with a purpose. As with many financial decisions in my life up until then, my decision to save wasn't something intentional. Saving money was something I simply believed people were supposed to do. Like buying a house or paying cash for a car; saving seemed like the responsible thing that adults do.

Beyond saving, though, I never took the time to educate myself on what my money could do for me or my family. I always assumed I would serve 20 plus years, earn a pension, retire from the military, and then find some sort of second career to see my family through to proper retirement age (i.e. 65). Thus, investing my money for maximum effect never entered my thought pattern. The idea that I may need it if I reached a point where I no longer wished to serve never occurred to me. As already stated, that willful financial ignorance played heavily into my decision to deploy to Afghanistan in December 2012.

Golden Albatross Explained...Again

I've appropriated a term from the Internet for the inflection point that many people who work in pensionable career fields inevitably hit. It's the point where they must decide if pressing onward to their pension is actually *worth it*, and I call it the *Golden Albatross*. That term represents both the blessing and the curse that is a Defined Benefit Pension (DBP). Like the albatross around the neck of the Ancient Mariner, the sacrifice and determination that a pensionable career often requires can weigh heavy. So heavy in fact, that people may develop serious mental or physical health issues as they toil onwards to completion. It's not always like that, but it certainly happens to some.

On the other hand, the security in retirement that a DBP represents is hard to walk away from...even when the career causes mental or physical pain and suffering. Certainly, some pensions are worth more than others. That calculus depends on numerous factors I won't bother to explain here but is easy enough to research online. For those of us in the U.S. military, the ironclad safety provided by a federal pension makes it hard to turn down after a certain number of years of service. Thus, the golden aspect of the albatross metaphor.

Golden Albatross inflection points differ from person to person depending on the circumstances. For some unfortunate percentage who fail to save and invest, there will be no choice—they must continue until they become pension-eligible. Even then, a second career may not be enough to save them from their continued bad financial decisions. Others find that no amount of monetary compensation is worth the continued cost of work in their current pensionable field. Thus, they look for other options and make their move at the appropriate time...or when they can't take it anymore. For yet another percentage, working until pensionable age is not only easy but all they ever want to do. A large percentage of the rest probably fall somewhere in the middle— happy to do the job (or in our case serve) until they no longer enjoy it.

Unfortunately for me, I blew through my real *Golden Albatross* moment at 13 years of service in December 2012 without realizing it. How could I? Since I always assumed I was in the military for the long haul, the term *Golden Albatross*, let alone the concept, wasn't even in my vocabulary. There was no thought of finishing out in the reserves or looking for a civilian career. My misplaced belief that my savings didn't allow me to face a Continuation Board without fear for my family's future financial stability virtually guaranteed I would deploy.

On the Way Down

Acting out of financial ignorance and fear doesn't typically end well, and it certainly didn't for me. By the time I mentally broke down in 2016 (17 years into my career), there was no real *Golden Albatross* decision to make. Even though I wanted to leave, I felt compelled to stay for the pension. When I ran the numbers on the Department of Defense's retirement calculator page and saw how much I would lose if I resigned, it sealed the deal. The sum was literally in the millions of dollars in future pension payments.

Therefore, my decision was not *if* my pension was worth it, but *how* to maintain my sanity while I stuck it out three more years. It was a truly horrible, and mercenary, feeling. I hadn't joined the military for the pension. I joined because I wanted to serve and give something back. However, in the end, I stayed...for the money.

Discovery of FI

Fortunately, all was not lost. Two years before my breakdown, I had started a personal finance journey—possibly spurred by a subconscious brain that knew all was not well. Thus, only months after my breakdown, be it through serendipity or divine intervention, I discovered the concept of Financial Independence (FI) as well as the Financial Independence Retire Early (FIRE) movement. For the uninitiated, Wikipedia states that:

> **Financial independence** *means you have enough wealth to live on without working. Financially independent people have assets that generate income (cash flow) that is at least equal to their expenses.*

FIRE is simply the term for the people who follow through with retirement from "a real job" after achieving FI. While some choose to never work again, many others choose to do something they love without consideration for the need to generate money. That may include volunteer work, blogging, arts, or any number of passion projects made possible by the end of a W-2 career.

Some of you may be skeptical and believe it takes millions of dollars for a person to achieve FI. I can understand the skepticism because I was skeptical, too, until I did the research and the math. The key to FI is in the definition, and it's the term *"at least equal to their expenses."* Every person or family spends a certain amount of money to live a happy life based on their values and judgment of wants versus needs. For some, that may be $40,000. For others, it may be $400,000. It's different for everybody but the lower a person or family can make that number, the fewer assets they need to accumulate to generate the cash flow required to cover the expenses.

Now, in what I call the *mainstream* FI movement there's typically a combination of two ways to achieve FI—frugality and the accumulation of assets. Some choose to emphasize one path over the other, possibly to the extreme. Yet most people find some sort of happy middle ground that works for them. That may include a medium-sized investment portfolio and a modest lifestyle. Or it may include a rental real estate empire and an upper-class lifestyle in a high cost of living area. Honestly, the interplay between the types of assets accumulated, versus the management of expenses, to achieve FI, are almost endless.

A Brief History of Pensions

However, I'm here to tell you there's a third way for the pensioner. In fact, it used to be the *primary* way people achieved FI. Before the 1980s in the U.S., a company or government Defined Benefit Pension (DBP) was potentially all a person or family needed for retirement. Certainly, a DBP in conjunction with social security and a moderate amount of savings in a high-interest savings account saw millions of people across the FI goal line by retirement age.

Times have changed, though. The Defined Benefit Pension is an anachronism. They are only found in a few hold-out industries which are typically unionized, or government work at the Federal, State, and Local level. The primary reason for the decline of DBPs is their expense. In a day and age when people are living longer, paying them to not work from their voluntary or mandatory retirement age until death incurs a future cost that most companies and many governments cannot afford. Couple the exploding costs of healthcare to a pension, and the expense grows even faster.

These factors drove the transition from DBPs to the Defined Contribution (DC) system in the U.S. in the 1980s and 1990s. That trend continues to this day. For those who don't know, a DC system is typically based around a 401(k), or some other tax-deferred savings/investment vehicle sponsored by an employer.

The rise of the DC system for retirement represents a transfer of risk—specifically, the risk of running out of money in the future—from the large organization to the individual. On the other hand, the upside of DC plans includes their transferability. This allows workers to take the value of the DC plan with them whenever they change employers. As a result, *Golden Albatross* moments are almost non-existent for the majority of U.S. workers these days. If they decide they don't like their current job, they can simply switch without agonizing over it and take their retirement money with them.

The Gap Number

As already mentioned, only a few industries, companies, or govern-ments currently provide pensions. The hold-out career fields often require some sort of sacrifice; be it potential life and limb, or forgone earnings due to government pay scales, or both. On one hand, pensions can be viewed as an expensive tool that entices workers to stay in a job when it may not be in their best interest to do so. However, looked at differently, they are also a tool that provides a serious boost to anyone looking to achieve either FI or FIRE. This certainly includes those of us in the U.S. military who make it to pensionable age.

In personal finance terms, a pension typically provides an *income floor* that a retiree will (hopefully) never fall below. The more of their mandatory and discretionary expenses a retiree can cover with their pension, the less income they require from their other accumulated assets. This, in turn, translates to a smaller total nest egg required for retirement. In other words, the smaller a person can make this gap between their projected retirement expenses and fixed-income, the more easily they can achieve FI. Ideally, a pension would cover all mandatory and discretionary expenses to include healthcare. However, that's no guarantee these days. Certainly, though, the goal for future pensioners seeking FI should be to make their *Gap Number* as small as possible.

FIRE...in My Belly

As I struggled to recover from my mental breakdown in mid-to-late 2016, I started educating myself with as many FI related books and blogs as I could read. Then I started to make some calculations. With the assistance of 16 years' worth of spending data stored in my preferred money tracking program, I ran my projected retirement expenses, including the benefits of a DoD retirement with its subsidized healthcare. In doing so, I had an epiphany. I realized that with a few adjustments to our savings, and a sound retirement plan, that FIRE was a real possibility for me and my family. More importantly, *it was obtainable with as few as 20 years of service.*

I can honestly say that my FIRE realization did more to alleviate my PTS linked anxiety than any amount of therapy up to that point. It didn't solve the depression, but it still transformed my mental state for the better. The simple realization that in three short years I could move beyond the need to ever work for money again nearly made the Afghanistan deployment and its aftermath worth it...nearly. Although not totally healed, I'm certainly in a much better mental state today than I was a few years ago. A big reason for that is my FI and personal finance realization.

Speaking of personal finance, it's important to note that all the saving over the years, while not directed towards anything specific, helped tremendously when it came time to make my retirement calculations work. More importantly, through deliberate financial planning, my family's effort to save money in the future has a clear purpose. It's not as if we *sacrifice* all that much either. My two children want for nothing, although we certainly don't spoil them with material possessions. We rent a nice house in a nice neighborhood, and we travel whenever we want. Yet, we still net a 25-35% savings rate, just as we've done for many years.

My Financial Tools

All this talk of personal finance reminds me of the financial tools I intend to leave with you today. The first is my list of seven financial guidelines. The guidelines are:

 Track your money

 Don't spend more than you earn

 Save a significant amount of what you earn

 Eliminate or avoid (consumer) debt

 Proactively educate yourself on personal finance

 Deliberately plan for your financial future

 Invest

The list is nothing groundbreaking or new. It's mostly just financial common sense. However, it's the type of common sense I wish someone had pounded into my skull much earlier in my career. I purposely call them guidelines as a nod to the *Pirates of the Caribbean* joke about rules vs. guidelines in the Pirate's Code. Other than the first guideline, I'm not even convinced in what order they should flow. You could easily employ several of them concurrently.

Yes, the guidelines are vague for a reason. Take *invest* as an example. Notice I don't tell you what to invest in. That's a personal decision that requires some education on your part. Several of you may choose low-cost index funds, while others might choose real estate. Others still may prefer picking individual stocks or bonds. There is no one-size-fits-all process. Instead, I simply advise that you consider the guidelines and apply them appropriately to fit your life and career.

The other two financial tools I leave with you are a pair of decision trees built around the idea of the *Golden Albatross* moment. (See the end of the chapter resources for Chapter 13) I designed the first decision tree to assist people with answering the "Is the pension *worth it?*" question. I designed the other decision tree to assist people if they decide "yes" to the first question. Like the guidelines, these decision trees are based on financial common sense. I'd be happy to take any questions you may have on these tools.

Unicorns and Rainbows

With all that said, my parting thought for you is this: Despite everything I've discussed today, I remain extremely grateful for the opportunity to serve. Military service was my dream since the age of six. I never wanted to do anything else. Yet, as happens in life, my priorities changed over time. The need to serve gave way to a need to be there for my family. Unfortunately for me, I never prepared properly for that change. I compounded that mistake by ignoring my mounting mental health issues. As a result, everything crashed down on me at once.

That mental crash was my fault. It remains my burden to bear, but it doesn't have to be yours. I hope that none of you need to put any of this "be prepared just in case" financial advice to use. I'd rather you serve 20 or more blissful years, get out with nothing but great memories, a better pension, a fat bank account, and the option to do anything you want with the rest of your life. I hope that one day you can joke with your classmates about that crazy officer who tried to scare all of you with his personal finance horror story.

However, I regret to inform you that most military careers don't end with unicorns and rainbows, which is why I urge each of you to plan now in case your experience starts to sour. Give yourself options, even if you never intend to use them. Consider alternative paths and plan financial goals to make them viable. That way you'll never find yourself stuck in the belief, as I was, that you have no options.

2019 Epilogue

I wrote the above portion of this speech about a year ago. As often happens, life changed majorly in the intervening time-frame. First and foremost, I decided to retire at 20-years of service, instead of waiting until I was eligible to transfer my GI Bill at 21-years. My decision to retire was a conscious one and centered on the fact that I continued to struggle with several health problems including the continued effects of stress. When I made the decision to stay in 2016, I knowingly elected a path that might cause more permanent damage to my health. At the time though, I thought I could cope with any additional stress through the help of therapy and medication.

However, by the time I crossed the 19-year mark, it was apparent to me that I was both unable and unwilling to continue to operate in the high-stress environment that is today's military. Like an aged professional athlete, I realized I no longer had the heart or the ability to compete at the championship level. So, I called my final shot and dropped my retirement letter with a final date to coincide with my Projected Rotation Date (PRD) for my current set of orders. As a result, I'm speaking to you only months before I start my terminal leave.

As just mentioned, my decision to retire at 20-years was a conscious one and represented a major change to my earlier retirement plan. It's important to note that I only made the decision after running the financial numbers. I specifically wanted to know if forgoing the transfer of the GI Bill would place my family at future financial risk. My simulations said no, and that my family would be fine. As a result, I pulled the retirement trigger.

The other thing I did was re-energize my mental health treatment. I started by working with my doctors to ramp down from the anti-anxiety/anti-depression medication I'd used for over two-years. I did that for several reasons. Primarily, I wanted to see if I still needed medication. If not, then one less thing to worry about. On the other hand, if I discovered that I still needed it, I wanted to try a different prescription. I hated the side effects of that medication. Thus, if I had to take medication long-term, I wanted to switch to a medication with fewer side-effects.

I'm glad I ran that experiment with my medical support structure in place because it failed. I discovered I'm barely functional under stress without medication. My issues started to impact my work and sent my family life into a tailspin. It wasn't easy, but I made it down the off-ramp from my previous medication, and safely transitioned to a new one.

Despite the bumpy road, going through that ordeal was worth it, because it helped me realize exactly how much further I need to progress to get better—if I ever do. In the meantime, the stress at work hasn't abated. If anything, it's only ratcheted-up in the past few months. As a result, I feel like I'm falling behind in my retirement preparations.

Not only that, but retirement planning got a lot more complicated when my wife and I started to seriously consider emigrating to New Zealand after my retirement. This translates into stress at home as we deal with the uncertainties of the visa and emigration process. It's a far cry from the San Diego retirement plan I prepared and refined over the past few years. I believe we could easily execute the San Diego plan with much less stress, but it holds a lot less upside potential for doing something truly different and amazing with the remainder of our lives. For the moment, between the medication and therapy, I'm just about able to cope.

This is all to say that I'm still a work in progress, and so is my personal, family, and financial life. I definitely don't have it all figured out. The entire story I just related to you is still evolving. It's evolving because I've worked hard in my late-career to create choices and options for myself and my family for our post-military life. The truth of the matter is San Diego or New Zealand are two pretty sweet choices— but they didn't come about easily. My hope, in fact, the entire point of this speech (and this book), is that you learn from my mistakes and build better options and easier paths without all the pain and sacrifice I endured.

Thank you for your time.

Interested in contacting Grumpus Maximus with questions, comments, or concerns?

He can be reached

via email at grumpusmaximus@grumpusmaximus.com

via Facebook under Grumpus Maximus

via Twitter @maximusgrumpus

or on Instagram at grumpusmaximustoo

Bibliography

Introduction

Kagan, J. (2019) "Defined Benefit Plan." *Investopedia*. Online. Available at https://www. investopedia.com/terms/d/definedbenefitpensionplan.asp/ . Updated 7/30/2019

Chapter 1– What is a Golden Albatross?

Kagan, J. (2019) "Defined Benefit Plan." *Investopedia*. Online. Available at https://www. investopedia.com/terms/d/definedbenefitpensionplan.asp/ . Updated 7/30/2019

"Golden Handcuffs" *Wikipedia*. Online. Available at https://en.wikipedia.org/wiki/Golden_ handcuffs . Visited 1/17/2020

Zaleski, A. (2015) "The Rembrandts' 'I'll Be There For You' was a golden albatross." *AV Club*. Online. Available at https://music.avclub.com/the-rembrandts-i-ll-be-there-for-you-was-a-golden-al-1798280808 . 6/11/2015

Chapter 2 – Worth vs. Worth It

McKay, B & McKay,K. (2014) "Be a Time Wizard: How to Slow Down and Speed Up Time." *Art of Manliness*. Online. Available at https://www.artofmanliness.com/articles/be-a-time-wizard-how-to-slow-down-and-speed-up-time/ 8/11/2014

Chapter 3 – Why Would One Stay?

Collins, J (2016) *The Simple Path to Wealth*

"The Simple Path to Wealth | Mad Fientist Interview" *Mad Fientist*. Online. Available at https://www.madfientist.com/jl-collins-interview/ . 6/21/2016

"You Can Teach an Old Dog New Tricks." Online. Available at https://grumpusmaximus.com/you-can-teach-an-old-dog-new-tricks/ . 8/12/2017

"An Unintentional Meander up Grumpy Avenue (Part 1)." Online. Available at https://grumpusmaximus.com/an-unintentional-meander-up-grumpy-avenue-part-1/ . 7/2/2017

"Retirement Planning: How to Calculate Your Gap Number." Online. Available at https://grumpusmaximus.com/retirement-planning-how-to-calculate-your-gap-number/ . 7/24/2017

"Financial Planning (Part 2): The GRO2W Plan." Online. Available at https://grumpusmaximus.com/financial-planning-part-ii-the-gro2w-plan/ . 6/27/2017

"FI Numbers Don't Lie, But They May Mislead (Part 1)." Online. Available at https://grumpusmaximus.com/fi-numbers-may-mislead-part-1/ 8/19/2017

Chapter 4 – Gutting It Out

Lee, T., Horn, P., Eberly, M., Li, J. (2018)"Managing employee retention and turnover with 21st century ideas" *Organizational Dynamics*. Available online at https://www.sciencedirect.com/science/article/abs/pii/S0090261617301833?via%3Dihub

Clark, A., Oswald, A., Warr, P. (1996) "Is job satisfaction U-shaped in age?" *Journal of Occupational and Organizational Psychology*. Printed in Great Britain in 1996. Available online at https://www.andrewoswald.com/docs/jooparticle.pdf

Beard, A, and Setiya, K. (2019) "How to Cope With a Mid-Career Crisis." *Harvard Business Review*. Online. Available at https://hbr.org/ideacast/2019/02/how-to-cope-with-a-mid-career-crisis . 2/12/2019

Malito, A. (2018) "Miserable in your 40s? Don't Panic, it's Perfectly Normal." *Marketwatch*. Online. Available at https://www.marketwatch.com/story/miserable-in-your-40s-dont-panic-its-perfectly-normal-2018-07-10 . 7/11/2018

"Antoine de Saint-Exupéry" *Goodreads*. Online. Available at https://www.goodreads.com/author/show/1020792.Antoine_de_Saint_Exup_ry

"Test Your Retirement Plan: FI Numbers Don't Lie, But ... (Part 2)." Online. Available at https://grumpusmaximus.com/fi-numbers-part-2-test-your-retirement-plan/ . 8/27/2017

Morrissey, M. (2016) "The Power of Writing Down Your Goals and Dreams" *Huffington Post*. Online. Available at https://www.huffingtonpost.com/marymorrissey/the-power-of-writing-down_b_12002348.html Updated 12/6/2017

Pros, D. (2015) "5 Reasons Why Writing Down Goals Increases The Odds Of Achieving Them" *Elite Daily*. Online. Available at https://www.elitedaily.com/money/writing-down-your-goals/1068863 . 6/30/2015

"Americans need to take a break" *The Economist*. Online. Available at https://www.economist.com/business/2018/11/24/americans-need-to-take-a-break . 11/24/2018

"State of American Vacation 2018" *US Travel*. Online. Available at https://projecttimeoff.com/reports/state-of-american-vacation-2018/ . 5/8/2018

Scribner, H. (2014) "7 benefits of taking vacation time" *Deseret News*. Online. Available at https://www.deseretnews.com/article/865609183/7-benefits-of-taking-vacation-time.html . 8/20/2014

Gilbert, F. (2017) "A 10-Day Retirement." *Retirement Manifesto*. Online. Available at https://www.theretirementmanifesto.com/a-10-day-retirement/ . 12/5/2017

"Sunk Costs: The Charlie Brown E-Bike Blues." Online. Available at https://grumpusmaximus.com/sunk-costs-charlie-brown-e-bike-blues/ . 11/29/2017

Chapter 5 – The Opposite of Gutting It Out

Schrager, A. (2017) "Only one in five people take up this incredibly generous pension to retire at 40" QZ. Online. Available at https://qz.com/929153/only-one-in-five-people-take-up-this-incredibly-generous-pension-to-retire-at-40/ . 3/14/2017

"Multi-Task Your Way to Financial Independence (FI)" Online. Available at https://grumpusmaximus.com/multi-task-your-way-to-financial-independence-fi/ . 6/28/2017

Tardi, C. (2019) "Vested Benefit Definition." *Investopedia*. Online. Available at https://www.investopedia.com/terms/v/vested-benefit.asp . Updated 7/10/2019

"3 Books + 2 Booklets + 1 Chapter = Financial Independence (FI)" Online. Available at https://grumpusmaximus.com/3-books-2-booklets-1-chapter-financial-independence-fi/ . 6/27/2017

"TRANSITION ASSISTANCE PROGRAM (TAP) FOR MILITARY PERSONNEL" United States Department of Defence. Online. Available at https://www.esd.whs.mil/Portals/54/Documents/DD/issuances/dodi/133235p.pdf?ver=2018-11-08-133557-850 . Effective 9/26/2019

Chapter 6 – Mental Health, Sad Work, and Stuff

"An Unintentional Meander up Grumpy Avenue (Part 1)." Online. Available at https://grumpusmaximus.com/an-unintentional-meander-up-grumpy-avenue-part-1/ . 7/2/2017

"The Pension Series (Part 5): Survivorship (Updated)" Online. Available at https://grumpusmaximus.com/pension-series-part-5-survivorship/ . 1/16/2018

"Work and Mental Health: Slaying the Dragon" Online. Available at https://grumpusmaximus.com/work-and-mental-health-slaying-dragon/ . 12/3/2017

"Mercenary" *Merriam Webster*. Online. Available at https://www.merriam-webster.com/dictionary/mercenary . Visited 1/17/2020

"Article 47 - Mercenaries." International Committee of the Red Cross. Online. Available at https://ihl-databases.icrc.org/applic/ihl/ihl.nsf/ART/470-750057?OpenDocument . Effective 6/8/1977

Collins, J. (2011) "Why you need F-you money" Online. Available at http://jlcollinsnh.com/2011/06/06/why-you-need-f-you-money/ . Visited 1/17/2020

Barrett, B and Mendonsa, J. "The Why of FI" *ChooseFI*. Online. Available at https://www.choosefi.com/038-the-why-of-fi/ . 9/22/2017

Collins, J (2016) *The Simple Path to Wealth*

"Go Fever" *Wikipedia*. Online. Available at https://en.wikipedia.org/wiki/Go_fever . Visited 1/17/2020

Barrett, B and Mendonsa, J. "Design Your Future with Dominick Quartuccio " *ChooseFI*. Online. Available at https://www.choosefi.com/033-design-future/ . 7/24/2017

"Multi-Task Your Way to Financial Independence (FI)" Online. Available at https://grumpusmaximus.com/multi-task-your-way-to-financial-independence-fi/ . 6/28/2017

"3 Books + 2 Booklets + 1 Chapter = Financial Independence (FI)" Online. Available at https://grumpusmaximus.com/3-books-2-booklets-1-chapter-financial-independence-fi/ . 6/27/2017

"5 + 1 Financial Independence Blogsites (Besides Mine) You Should Check Out." Online. Available at https://grumpusmaximus.com/5-1-financial-independence-blogsites-besides-mine-you-should-check-out/ . 6/25/2017

"Mental Health: Sad Work and Stuff." Online. Available at https://grumpusmaximus.com/mental-health-sad-work-stuff/ . 1/21/2018

Barrett, B and Mendonsa, J. "The Golden Albatross" *ChooseFI*. Online. Available at https://www.choosefi.com/057-the-golden-albatross-grumpus-maximus/ . 1/8/2018

Chapter 7 – Is Your Pension Safe?

"Employee Contributions to Public Pension Plans" NASRA. Online. Available at https://www.nasra.org/files/Issue%20Briefs/NASRAContribBrief.pdf . 9/1/2019

"Actuarial Science" *Wikipedia*. Online. Available at https://en.wikipedia.org/wiki/Actuarial_science . Visited 1/17/2020

"The 80% Pension Funding Standard Myth" American Academy of Actuaries. Online. Available at https://www.actuary.org/files/80_Percent_Funding_IB_071912.pdf . 7/19/2012

Segal, T. (2019) "7 Things You Didn't Know About Sovereign Defaults" *Investopedia*. Online. Available at http://www.investopedia.com/financial-edge/0911/7-things-you-didnt-know-about-sovereign-debt-defaults.aspx Updated 5/25/2019

Roming, S. (2014) "Argentina's Long History of Economic Booms and Busts" *The Wall Street Journal*. Online. Available at https://blogs.wsj.com/moneybeat/2014/07/30/argentinas-long-history-of-economic-booms-and-busts/ . 7/30/2014

Loftus, T. (2017) "Pension crisis: Workers swamp KRS with questions" Courier Journal. Online. Available at http://www.courier-journal.com/story/news/politics/2017/09/01/kentucky-pension-crisis-workers-seek-retirement-information/625592001/ . 9/1/2017

Meisler, I. (2017) "Pension Fund Problems Worsen in 43 States:" Bloomberg. Online. Available at https://www.bloomberg.com/graphics/2017-state-pension-funding-ratios/ . Updated 8/29/2017

Kagan, J. (2019) "Defined Benefit Plan." *Investopedia*. Online. Available at https://www.investopedia.com/terms/d/definedbenefitpensionplan.asp/ . Updated 7/30/2019

"Pension Series (Part 14): Pension Risk Transfer." Online. Available at https://grumpusmaximus.com/pension-series-14-pension-risk-transfer/ . 5/23/2018

McGrath, C. (2018). "The rise of pension risk transfers" *Pensions and Investments*. Online. Available at https://www.pionline.com/article/20180806/INTERACTIVE/180809922/graphic-the-rise-of-pension-risk-transfers/W . 8/6/2018

Constable, S.(2017) "Corporate Pension Funding Gap To Hit Record This Year" *Forbes*. Online. Available at https://www.forbes.com/sites/simonconstable/2017/08/11/corporate-pension-funding-cap-to-hit-record-this-year/ . 8/11/2017

White, R. (2019) "Is Your Defined-Benefit Pension Plan Safe?" *Investopedia*. Online. Available at https://www.investopedia.com/articles/retirement/08/safe-db-plan.asp . 11/27/2019

"Financial Planning (Part 1): Time and Planning" Online. Available at http://www.grumpusmaximus.com/financial-planning-part-1-time-and-planning/ . 6/25/2017

"Test Your Retirement Plan: FI Numbers Don't Lie, But ... (Part 2)" Online. Available at http://www.grumpusmaximus.com/fi-numbers-part-2-test-your-retirement-plan/ . 8/27/2017

Anspach, D. (2019) "What is a Pension and How Do You Get One?" *The Balance*. Online. Available at https://www.thebalance.com/pensions-4073064. 8/15/2019

Palmer, B. (2019) "Why Might Your 401(k) Be Unavailable After You Leave a Job?" *Investopedia*. Online. Available at http://www.investopedia.com/articles/retirement/10/signs-pension-fund-trouble.asp . 12/9/2019

Wayman, R. (2019) "The Investing Risk of Underfunded Pension Plans" *Investopedia*. Online. Available at http://www.investopedia.com/articles/analyst/03/050803.asp . 7/9/2019

Silverblatt, H. (2017). "S&P 500® Corporate Pension and Other Post-Employment Benefits (OPEB) in 2017" *S&P 500 Indices*. Online. Available at https://us.spindices.com/documents/research/research-sp-500-corporate-pensions-and-OPEB-in-2017.pdf . Visited 1/17/2020

"Pension Series (Part 14): Pension Risk Transfer." Online. Available at https://grumpusmaximus.com/pension-series-14-pension-risk-transfer/ . 5/23/2018

"The Pension Series (Part 15): The Pension Benefit Guaranty Corporation (PBGC)" Online. Available at https://grumpusmaximus.com/pension-series-15-pbgc/ . 6/11/2018

Chapter 8 – What's Your Pension Worth?

Kagan, J. (2019) "Defined Benefit Plan." *Investopedia*. Online. Available at https://www.investopedia.com/terms/d/definedbenefitpensionplan.asp/ . Updated 7/30/2019

"Vest" Financial Dictionary. Online. Available at https://financial-dictionary.thefreedictionary.com/vest . Visited 1/17/2020

Chen, J. (2019) "Cliff Vesting Definition" *Investopedia*. Online. Available at https://www.investopedia.com/terms/c/cliffvesting.asp . Updated 4/12/2019

Fontinelle, A. (2019) "Pension Vesting: Everything You Need to Know" *Investopedia*. Online. Available at https://www.investopedia.com/retirement/pension-vesting-everything-you-need-know/ . Updated 12/12/2019

"Overview of BLS Statistics on Inflation and Prices" *United States Bureau of Labor Statistics*. Online. Available at https://www.bls.gov/bls/inflation.htm . Visited 1/17/2020

"Star Wars: Episode IV - A New Hope" *Box Office Mojo*. Online. Available at https://www.boxofficemojo.com/releasegroup/gr22499845/ .Visited 1/17/2020

"Box Office History for Star Wars Movies" *The Numbers*. Online. Available at https://www.the-numbers.com/movies/franchise/Star-Wars#tab=summary&franchise_movies_overview=od4.Visited 1/17/2020

"Star Wars: Episode VII - The Force Awakens" *Box Office Mojo*. Online. Available at https://www.boxofficemojo.com/title/tt2488496/?ref_=bo_se_r_1 . Visited 1/17/2020

Manual, D. "What Did It Cost? A Look Back" Online. Available at https://www.davemanuel.com/whatitcost.php . Visited 1/17/2020

Howard, R. "Purchasing Power Calculator" *Buy Upside*. Online. Available at https://www.buyupside.com/calculators/purchasepowerjan08.htm . Visited 1/17/2020

"12-month percentage change, Consumer Price Index, selected categories" *United States Bureau of Labor Statistics*. Online. Available at https://www.bls.gov/charts/consumer-price-index/consumer-price-index-by-category-line-chart.htm . Visited 1/17/2020

Howard, R. "Inflation Calculator" *Buy Upside*. Online. Available at http://www.buyupside.com/calculators/inflationjan08.htm . Visited 1/17/2020

"Exponentiation". *Study.com*. Online. Available at https://study.com/academy/lesson/exponentiation-definition-examples-quiz.html . Visited 1/17/2020

Anspach, D. (2019) "Determining a Safe Retirement Withdrawal Rate" *The Balance*. Online. Available at https://www.thebalance.com/withdrawal-rate-retirement-planning-2388685 . Updated 8/1/2019

Pfua, W. "The 4% Rule And The Search For A Safe Withdrawal Rate" *The Retirement Researcher*. Online. Available at https://retirementresearcher.com/the-4-rule-and-the-search-for-a-safe-withdrawal-rate/. Visited 1/17/2020

"Retirement Planning: How to Calculate Your Gap Number." Online. Available at https://grumpusmaximus.com/retirement-planning-how-to-calculate-your-gap-number/ . 7/24/2017

Anspach, D. (2019) "Sequence Risk's Impact on Your Retirement Money" *The Balance*. Online. Available at https://www.thebalance.com/how-sequence-risk-affects-your-retirement-money-2388672 . Updated 2/8/2019

"The Pension Series (Part 7): How to Create Your Own COLA" Online. Available at https://grumpusmaximus.com/pension-series-part-7-create-cola/ . 10/29/2017

Jeske, K. "The Ultimate Guide to Safe Withdrawal Rates – Part 4: Social Security and Pensions" *Early Retirement Now*. Online. Available at https://earlyretirementnow.com/2017/01/04/the-ultimate-guide-to-safe-withdrawal-rates-part-4-social-security-pensions/. Visited 1/17/2020

"The Pension Series (Part 18): Social Security – The People's Pension" Online. Available at https://grumpusmaximus.com/pension-series-part-18-social-security/ . 12/16/2018

"Flexible Retirement Planner"Online. Available at https://www.flexibleretirementplanner.com/wp/ . Visited 1/17/2020

Chapter 9 – How To Determine Your Pension's Total Dollar Value (TDV)

"10 Common Causes Of Errors In Pension Calculation" *United States Department of Labor*. Online. Available at https://www.dol.gov/agencies/ebsa/about-ebsa/our-activities/resource-center/publications/10-common-causes-of-errors-in-pension-calculation . Visited 1/17/2020

"The Pension Series (Part 5): Survivorship (Updated)" Online. Available at https://grumpusmaximus.com/pension-series-part-5-survivorship/ . 1/16/2018

"H.R. 4280 (98th): Retirement Equity Act of 1984" *GovTrack*. Online. Available at https://www.govtrack.us/congress/bills/98/hr4280. Visited 1/17/2020

"The Pension Series (Part 8): Deciding to Take a Pension Lump Sum" Online. Available at https://grumpusmaximus.com/pension-series-part-8-pension-lump-sum/ . 11/13/2017

"Military Compensation" *United States Department of Defence*. Online. Available at https://militarypay.defense.gov/Calculators.aspx . Visited 1/17/2020

"Retirement & Survivors Benefits: Life Expectancy Calculator" United States Social Security Administration. Online. Available at https://www.ssa.gov/OACT/population/longevity.html . Visited 1/17/2020

Howard, R. "Inflation Calculator" *Buy Upside*. Online. Available at http://www.buyupside.com/calculators/inflationjan08.htm . Visited 1/17/2020

Howard, R. "Growing Annuity Due Calculator - Future Value" *Buy Upside*. Online. Available at https://www.buyupside.com/calculators/annuitygrowingduefuturevalue.htm . Visited 1/17/2020

Pal, T. "Future Value of Annuity Calculator" *OmniCalculator*. Online. Available at https://www.omnicalculator.com/finance/annuity-future-value#how-to-use-our-annuity-calculator . Visited 1/17/2020

Jeske, K. "The Ultimate Guide to Safe Withdrawal Rates – Part 17: More on Social Security and Pensions (and why we should call the 4% Rule the "4% Rule of Thumb")" *Early Retirement Now*. Online. Available at https://earlyretirementnow.com/2017/07/19/the-ultimate-guide-to-safe-withdrawal-rates-part-17-social-security/ . Visited 1/17/2020

Chapter 10 – How To Use This Newfound Knowledge

"Retirement Planning: How to Calculate Your Gap Number." Online. Available at https://grumpusmaximus.com/retirement-planning-how-to-calculate-your-gap-number/ . 7/24/2017

Berger, R. (2014) "3 Ways to Calculate Your Retirement Number" *U.S. News*. Online. Available at https://money.usnews.com/money/blogs/on-retirement/2014/11/06/3-ways-to-calculate-your-retirement-number . 11/6/2014

Laise, E. (2016) "Will You Really Need to Replace 80% of Your Preretirement Paycheck?" *Kiplinger*. Online. Available at https://www.kiplinger.com/article/retirement/T037-C000-S004-replace-80-of-preretirement-paycheck.html . 4/1/2016

Chen, J. (2019) "Time Value of Money (TVM)" *Investopedia*. Online. Available at https://www.investopedia.com/terms/t/timevalueofmoney.asp . Updated 9/25/2019

Baldwin, W. (2016) "Maximize Your Pension With This Calculator" *Forbes*. Online. Available at https://www.forbes.com/sites/baldwin/2016/01/10/maximize-your-pension-with-this-calculator/#504a6c7a48d5 . 1/10/2016

Roberts, L. (2017) "Opinion: Americans are still terrible at investing, annual study once again shows" *MarketWatch*. Online. Available at https://www.marketwatch.com/story/americans-are-still-terrible-at-investing-annual-study-once-again-shows-2017-10-19 . 10/21/2017

Maximus, G. Editor: Kirkpatrick, D. (2017) "Deciding Whether to Take a Pension Lump Sum: The 2 Opposing Methods" *Can I Retire Yet*. Online. Available at https://www.caniretireyet.com/pension-lump-sum-2-opposing-methods/ . 11/13/2017

Chapter 11 – Valuing Pension Subsidized Healthcare

Kagan, J. (2019) "Other Post-Retirement Benefits." *Investopedia*. Online. Available at http://www.investopedia.com/terms/o/otherbenefits.asp . Updated 1/10/2019

Bakalar, N. (2017) "Nearly 20 Million Have Gained Health Insurance Since 2010" *The New York Times*. Online. Available at https://www.nytimes.com/2017/05/22/health/obamacare-health-insurance-numbers-nchs.html . 5/22/2017

Eibner,C. and Nowak, S. (2018) "Understanding the Impact of the Elimination of the Individual Mandate Penalty" *The Commonwealth Fund*. Online. Available at https://www.commonwealthfund.org/blog/2018/understanding-impact-elimination-individual-mandate-penalty . 8/9/2018

Luhby, T. (2016) "Is Obamacare really affordable? Not for the middle class" *CNN*. Online. Available at https://money.cnn.com/2016/11/04/news/economy/obamacare-affordable/index.html . 11/4/2016

Squires, D. and Anderson, C. (2015) "U.S. Health Care from a Global Perspective" *The Commonwealth Fund*. Online. Available at https://www.commonwealthfund.org/publications/

issue-briefs/2015/oct/us-health-care-global-perspective?redirect_source=/publications/
issue-briefs/2015/oct/us-health-care-from-a-global-perspective . 10/8/2015

Mamula, C. (2017) "A Flexible Plan For Health Insurance In Early Retirement" *Can I Retire Yet?*
Online. Available at http://www.caniretireyet.com/flexible-health-insurance-early-retirement/ .
10/16/2017

Jeter, A. (2017) "What's the Near-Term Outlook for the Affordable Care Act?" *The Kaiser
Family Foundation.* Online. Available at https://www.kff.org/health-reform/press-release/
whats-the-near-term-outlook-for-the-affordable-care-act/ . 8/4/2017

Kirkpatrick, D. (2012) "Recurring Expenses: Why "A Dollar a Day" is Really $9,000" *Can I Retire
Yet?* Online. Available at http://www.caniretireyet.com/recurring-expenses-why-a-dollar-a-day-
is-really-9000/ . 3/6/2012

Gilbert, F. (2017) "Your 4 Biggest Worries About Retirement" *Retirement Manifesto.* Online.
Available at http://www.theretirementmanifesto.com/what-worries-you-the-most-about-
retirement/ . 9/12/2017

"Medical care prices rise 4 percent over the year ending November 2016" *United States
Bureau of Labor Statistics.* Online. Available at https://www.bls.gov/opub/ted/2016/medical-
care-prices-rise-4-percent-over-the-year-ending-november-2016.htm . 12/19/2016

Chapter 12 – The Grumpmatic and Mathemagic Comparison Methods

Maximus, G. Editor: Kirkpatrick, D. (2017) "Deciding Whether to Take a Pension Lump Sum:
The 2 Opposing Methods" *Can I Retire Yet?* Online. Available at http://www.caniretireyet.com/
pension-lump-sum-2-opposing-methods/ . 11/13/2017

Kennon, J. (2019) "What Is a Safe Retirement Withdrawal Rate?" *The Balance.* Online.
Available at https://www.thebalance.com/what-is-a-safe-retirement-withdrawal-rate-357223 .
Updated 6/25/2019

Anspach, D. (2019) "How the 4 Percent Rule Works in Retirement" *The Balance.* Online.
Available at https://www.thebalance.com/what-is-the-4percent-rule-in-retirement-2388273 .
Updated 11/6/2019

Jeske, K. "The Ultimate Guide to Safe Withdrawal Rates." *Early Retirement Now.* Online.
Available at https://earlyretirementnow.com/safe-withdrawal-rate-series/ Visited 1/17/2020

"Retirement Expert Wade Pfau on How Much Money You Really Need" *Chris Reining*. Online. Available at https://chrisreining.com/wade-pfau/. Visited 1/17/2020

"Bayes' Theorem" *Math is Fun*. Online. Available at https://www.mathsisfun.com/data/bayes-theorem.html . Visited 1/17/2020

Chapter 13 – A Golden Albatross Decision Aid

"Pension and FI Decision Trees." Online. Available at https://grumpusmaximus.com/pension-and-fi-decision-trees/ . 10/15/2017

Chapter 14 – Putting It All Together, The Golden Albatross Financial Philosophy

"Mental Health: Sad Work and Stuff." Online. Available at https://grumpusmaximus.com/mental-health-sad-work-stuff/ . 1/21/2018

"Pension Series (Part 2): Worth v Worth It." Online. Available at https://grumpusmaximus.com/pension-series-part-2-worth-vs-worth-it/ . 9/10/2017

"You Can Teach an Old Dog New Tricks." Online. Available at https://grumpusmaximus.com/you-can-teach-an-old-dog-new-tricks/ . 8/12/2017

"What is a Golden Albatross?" Online. Available at https://grumpusmaximus.com/what-is-a-golden-albatross/ .

"Financial Independence" *Wikipedia*. Online. Available at https://en.wikipedia.org/wiki/Financial_independence . Accessed 1/17/2020

"Pension Series (Part 1): Pension Safety." Online. Available at https://grumpusmaximus.com/pension-series-part-1-pension-safety/ . 9/3/2017.

"Pension Series (Part 14): Pension Risk Transfer." Online. Available at https://grumpusmaximus.com/pension-series-14-pension-risk-transfer/ . 5/23/2018

"Retirement Planning: How to Calculate Your Gap Number." Online. Available at https://grumpusmaximus.com/retirement-planning-how-to-calculate-your-gap-number/ . 7/24/2017

"Why I Trust my Plan for Now." Online. Available at https://grumpusmaximus.com/why-i-trust-my-plan-for-now/ . 3/5/2018

"Pension and FI Decision Trees." Online. Available at https://grumpusmaximus.com/pension-and-fi-decision-trees/ . 10/15/2017

"Retirement Anxiety: How I Retired Mine." Online. Available at https://grumpusmaximus.com/retirement-anxiety-how-i-retired-mine/ . 11/11/2018

CPSIA information can be obtained
at www.ICGtesting.com
Printed in the USA
BVHW030547040720
582952BV00002B/386